GATOR

GATOR

MY LIFE IN PINSTRIPES

RON GUIDRY

WITH ANDREW BEATON

CROWN
ARCHETYPE
NEW YORK

All rights reserved.
Published in the United States by Crown Archetype, an imprint of the
Crown Publishing Group, a division of Penguin Random House LLC,
New York.
crownpublishing.com

Crown Archetype and colophon is a registered trademark of
Penguin Random House LLC.

Library of Congress Cataloging-in-Publication Data is available upon
request.

ISBN 978-0-451-49930-1
Ebook ISBN 978-0-451-49932-5

Printed in the United States of America

Book design by Lauren Dong
Frontispiece courtesy of Brandon Guidry
Photograph of Guidry playing for the University of Southwestern Louisiana:
Baseball. 1971. Box N 06d–N 06f, Folder N 06d, Baseball 1971 L'Acadien.
Coll 1-N, University Archives Photographs. University Archives and
Acadiana Manuscripts Collection, Edith Garland Dupré Library, University
of Louisiana at Lafayette, Lafayette, Louisiana
Jacket design by Rachel Willey
Jacket photograph: New York Daily News Archive/Getty Images

10 9 8 7 6 5 4 3 2 1

First Edition

To my wife, Bonnie, for standing by my side and for your love,
patience, and encouragement;
my children, for allowing your father to fulfill
his childhood dream;
my teammates and coaches, for challenging me to be my best;
Mr. Steinbrenner and the Yankees organization,
for taking the chance; and
the Yankees fans, for your loyalty and acceptance.
I want you to know I heard you every time you cheered—
especially with two strikes.

CONTENTS

GATOR

1

THE GAME

*W*HERE'S GATOR!?"
George Steinbrenner's voice boomed through the clubhouse like a drill sergeant's at a marine corps boot camp. George always wanted to let you know how he felt. Sometimes he wanted to cuss at you. He liked it if you cussed back at him. He wanted to motivate you. To him, the cussing and the motivating were one and the same. It happened to so many guys, so many days. Especially this season. But this wasn't just any other day during the 1978 New York Yankees season. This was hours before the biggest game of the year. One of the biggest games in Yankees history. Arguably one of the biggest games in baseball history. George being George, the loudmouthed, pushy, in-your-face owner of the Yankees, he wanted to have words with his starting pitcher before the game. That starting pitcher was me. And I wanted none of it.

"*WHERE'S GATOR!?*" he bellowed.

It wasn't a question so much as a demand. If he wanted to talk to you, he expected an audience. In a couple of hours, we were set to play a one-game tiebreaker to decide the American League East. This was the first tiebreaker since baseball adopted divisions in 1969. And it wasn't against just any team. It was against the Boston Red Sox.

The game was straight out of a Hollywood script. Forget all of our internal mayhem from that season—the constant drama surrounding Reggie Jackson, the departure of our fiery and disagreeable manager, Billy Martin, and more. Boston against New York transcended all of that. There was the historical aspect: the Curse of the Bambino and the Red Sox spending decades, over half a century, nipping at our heels. There was what had happened this year: baseball's "Boston Massacre," in which the Red Sox led the division by fourteen games during the middle of the summer, only to give it away. Then, in the final week, they won eight in a row to tie it back up on the very last day. We were both 99-63. A coin was flipped, and the tiebreaker would be played at Fenway Park. A 163rd game in a 162-game season. One game to settle it all.

"WHERE'S GATOR!?"

My teammates didn't know where I was. Neither did our manager, Bob Lemon. Only one person in the clubhouse, our trainer, Gene Monahan, knew where I was hiding out. I had snuck into the training room to take a nap. I lay down beneath the training table, and Geno threw a couple of sheets over it so nobody could see me. People popped in and out of the clubhouse asking Geno if he had seen me. Geno shrugged and said he hadn't. When George got around to asking him, Geno said I might be collecting my thoughts out on the field. So off George went, furiously stomping around the dewy Fenway grass in search of his starting pitcher. Meanwhile, I was sound asleep.

I knew George would be coming for me. But I didn't need

anybody screaming at me. I knew exactly how big this game was; nobody had to remind me. So I didn't read the papers. If I was watching TV and a story about the game came up, I'd change the channel. I knew the entire country would be watching. Red Sox broadcaster Ned Martin said it best: "If there is anything going on in the world today," he mused, "I don't know what it is."

There were a bunch of reasons I could've been worried. Probably should've been worried. The Red Sox were every bit as good as us. The ninety-nine wins apiece said it all. Normally, ninety-nine wins would have won the division running away. Their lineup may have been the best in baseball. And they were red hot, winners of eight in a row. Moreover, the game was being played on their turf, Fenway Park. I was pitching on three days of rest, as opposed to my customary four. I knew I wouldn't have my best stuff.

But every step that had led me to this point in the season told me to ignore all of that. If you get caught up in it, you're likely to forget what your job is. I was brought up to be self-reliant and patient, something my long road to the majors reinforced, like crossbeams in a renovation. That's the reason I was here. The fact that I was able to take a nap underneath the training table two hours before the first pitch should tell you everything you need to know about how worried I was.

The 1978 Yankees season might have been the most famous soap opera in baseball history. The lead actors in the drama: owner George Steinbrenner, who fought and fired his manager, Billy Martin, after Billy told the press that Reggie Jackson and George deserved each other—"one's a born liar, the other's convicted." The manager who feuded with his players, suspending Reggie for five days after a game against Kansas City in which Reggie defied Billy by attempting to bunt. The players who butted heads with one another. The hurt feelings and catfights. The drama had a full complement of characters. Come to think of it, I'm not sure whether it was a soap opera or a three-ring circus. And it all took place on the biggest stage in sports, New York City, and on the most popular team in the history of America's national pastime. The fireworks and explosions rocked the entire country, on the front and back pages of the newspapers, on television, and on sports radio.

In the span of a couple of years I had gone from relative anonymity—a good old boy from Lafayette, Louisiana—to become the ace of the pitching staff. I knew the team depended on me, as much as anybody, to win. On the other hand, I was never the source of the team's drama. The reasons varied, but other folks—from Reggie to Billy to George to Sparky Lyle—were central figures of the discontent. I didn't have a beef with anybody. I tended to keep to myself and focus on doing my job in the best way I knew how. But that didn't mean I didn't observe what was going on. I was never far from it, but because I wasn't personally involved, I felt like I had the right distance to get some perspective about not just what happened but why it turned out the way it did—with us winning it all. You see, I'm not sure we would have won the World Series if all of that didn't go down. We may not have won if Billy remained our manager. We may not have won if our guys had issues but didn't hash them out.

The postmortems of the 1978 team centered on one fundamental question: How the heck did such a dysfunctional cast of stars and misfits manage to win it all? An ESPN mini-series about the team was called *The Bronx Is Burning*. My close friend Sparky Lyle wrote a book about the team, called *The Bronx Zoo,* that spent half a year on the bestseller lists. In other words, you wouldn't blame anyone for thinking that we had no business winning the World Series. You'd expect the story of the 1978 Yankees to be a narrative of a dysfunctional team going down in flames.

But that didn't happen. The way I see it, the 1978 Yankees didn't win *in spite* of what went down that season. We won *because* of what happened. A team that is willing to fight—even one another—can go one of two ways: into the toilet or into greatness. A team that is afraid of conflict can settle into complacency. That was not us. We were a team with the potential to be great. And I believe that out of all the craziness, we became a team that was both talented and fearless. We were hungry. We were relentless. We were fiercely competitive. And we came together as a team over the course of the season. I believe we were the smartest, most complete baseball team around. Far from dysfunctional, we did all the little things it takes to be great. And nowhere was all of that better demonstrated than in that playoff game against the Red Sox.

————

The day before, Sunday, October 1, the last day of the regular season, I was thinking about pitching on the next Tuesday in the first game of the playoffs, against Kansas City. We had won six in a row. Boston had won seven in a row. We led them by a game, so all we had to do was win our last game, against Cleveland, or have Boston lose, and we'd be in the playoffs. We were rolling, and we were playing against one of the worst teams in the league. But we lost the game 9–2. And when Boston beat Toronto 5–0, we were tied at ninety-nine wins apiece.

After we lost, I walked past Bob Lemon in the dugout and said, "I'll pitch tomorrow." I felt I had earned the right to decide that for myself—and the team. I had the most wins in baseball, twenty-four, against only three losses. My earned run average was the lowest in baseball; my nine shutouts, again, the most in baseball. Everyone told me I was a shoo-in to win the American League Cy Young. At that point, if I asked for the ball, I got it.

The only thing was, typically pitchers get four days of rest between starts. Pitching against Boston had me on three days of rest. And I had thrown my prior two starts on short rest, too. That was both good and bad. I had proven I could handle it. We won both games, and I had thrown a complete game each time. A total of eighteen innings, with six hits and just one run. But consecutive starts on short rest also meant my arm was even more taxed than usual.

The main thing I needed to think about was how the short rest would affect me. If the good Lord gave me the ability to throw ninety-five miles per hour, I would. At the same time, I knew I wouldn't be able to throw a hundred pitches at ninety-five. Maybe fifty or sixty pitches. That one less day of rest, for a power pitcher, meant a lot. But I knew I could still get people out, even the mighty Red Sox, at ninety-two miles per hour. I just had to be smart about what to throw, and where, and when to dial it up and down.

The only thing more important than me knowing all of that, though, was that my teammates did. Our catcher and captain, Thurman Munson, never said much to me about it.

He spoke up about matters when he needed to and otherwise didn't say shit that didn't need to be said. He didn't have to pat me on the butt and tell me to do this or do that. But he had faith in me, and I had faith in him, and together we knew we could navigate our way through it. And the players behind me on the field knew I wouldn't be throwing as hard as usual—so they adjusted their positioning. And as much as anything, those savvy adjustments won us the ball game.

Pitching in Fenway Park had never bothered me, honestly. Because of the Green Monster—the close, towering wall in left field—Fenway has a reputation for being tough on left-handed pitchers. But I knew I couldn't change the way I pitch because of the wall. Letting it get into my head, and trying to switch things up from what had been working for me all year, that's what could hurt me. In a one-game playoff, everything is as much mental as it is physical.

I didn't do anything different to prepare, because I had no time. By the time we lost on Sunday, and I decided that I'd pitch against Boston on Monday, there was nothing to do but get a good night's sleep and try to do what I had done all season. And what I had done during the season first and foremost was to put my mind at rest. In the last month I had pitched against Boston twice. Both games were complete-game, two-hit shutouts.

The first of those two, at Fenway, was part of what would be called "the Boston Massacre." Boston was nearly unbeatable at home that season, winning fifty-nine games and losing just twenty-two. Four of those losses came during that series. A four-game sweep of Boston, in Boston. It was unheard-of. You don't do something like that to the Boston Red Sox in their park. I read later that we hadn't swept the Red Sox in Fenway since 1949. We'd entered the series trailing them by four games in the division. We left it tied.

But it wasn't just that we won those four games. It was *how* we won, and the mental edge that we took from it. We scored forty-two runs in those four games. They put up only nine. They committed twelve errors in those four games. We made only five. We didn't just sweep them. We kicked their asses. Because of that, we weren't afraid to play them over there when they won the coin flip for the tiebreaker. It's not that we felt invincible—I know I didn't. But we sure had confidence that we could beat them. They were more afraid of us than we were of them. Never in my career had I gone into Boston with the same confidence I had going into that game.

That wasn't the issue, though. The thing was, we just didn't like 'em. But we had a lot of respect for the Sox, because they had a damn good team. As did we. It was a shame one of us had to lose.

———

That Monday, October 2, it was sunny and sixty-five degrees— perfect weather for baseball. It was a wonderful day for fans to come out and watch the game. Both sides had good hitting, good pitching, good defense. Games at Fenway are always special, given our long-standing rivalry, but day games are even more so. It's baseball in its classic, purest form.

The crowds in Boston were never *actually* huge. Fenway could only fit around 33,000 people at the time, about 20,000 fewer than Yankee Stadium. But nothing in Fenway felt small. The fans were loud and heckled you left and right. (Our fans do the same to their guys, I'm sure.) And while other, newer ballparks were bigger, that brought fans farther away from the field and the players. At Fenway, they're right on top of you. The seats overflowed with fans, and people spilled out into the aisles—33,000 Boston fans at Fenway felt like a million.

If the setting, the teams, the stakes, the season, didn't do enough to set the perfect stage, there was one other dimension: Boston's starting pitcher that day was Mike Torrez. For him, the game was personal. Torrez was a key part of us winning it all the previous year, 1977, when we got him in a trade from Oakland and he went on to win fourteen games for us and two games in the '77 World Series. But George didn't think he was valuable enough, or at least didn't want to pay him what he asked for, so after '77 he signed with Boston. Some said George tossed him aside too quickly, and Torrez did his best to prove that. He went on to win 16 games for Boston in '78. A seventeenth win, against his former team, would've been icing on the cake. I told him afterward that if he'd stayed with us, he would've been a 20-game winner, and we would've won 130 games. He laughed.

It's funny how things play out. I might never have been on the mound that day if we hadn't traded for Torrez the prior season. After we acquired him from Oakland, instead of flying directly to New York, he stopped in Montreal, where he was living at the time, to take care of some family matters. This was before cell phones. By the time the Yankees found out he had gone home, they had to scramble for a starting pitcher because Torrez was going to miss his first start for us. So Billy Martin turned to a lightly used left-hander he had spent the last year going out of his way to avoid using. That twenty-seven-year-old pitcher was me, and I threw eight and a third shutout innings against the Mariners that day. Now, a year and a half later, Torrez and I were about to take the mound against each other, with everything on the line.

————

In the first inning, I mowed down the first three batters. Two strikeouts, including one against Jim Rice, the MVP that season, whose forty-six home runs led the league. So did his 139 RBI. He played in every game that year for Boston—all 163. But for some reason, that season he hadn't been able to figure me out. The first game of my career was against Boston, and Rice was my first major-league strikeout. He made up for it later in the game—and, apart from that season, over the rest of our careers. We would play eleven more seasons against each other, and he finished batting .360 against me. Fact is, he could hit anybody—that's what took him to the Hall of Fame.

But he wasn't the only Hall of Famer in the Boston lineup. Carl Yastrzemski came up to lead off the bottom of the second inning. Yaz wasn't the player he'd once been, and as a lefty batter, he wasn't quite as good against left-handed pitchers like me. But he was still an All-Star, and players as good as Yaz make a living by taking advantage of pitchers who don't have their best stuff. Which I didn't. I was already running on fumes with the short rest. And the swing he took against me to start that inning—I don't know if you can even call it a swing—was something only he could pull off. I threw a pitch high and tight, and he chopped at it like he was wielding an axe. I had no idea how he was able to hit it. But he cracked it down the right-field line for a home run. Red Sox 1, Yankees 0.

Most games, I had the mentality that I wanted to throw a complete game and shut the other team out. That day, against Boston's lineup, on short rest, I knew I just had to keep us in the game. They had good hitters—but we did too. I just had to get deep enough to give our bullpen a chance to close it out. We had the finest relievers in the game with Goose Gossage and Sparky Lyle.

Yaz's homer sent the crowd into a frenzy, and when yet another future Hall of Famer, catcher Carlton Fisk, stepped to the plate the noise grew louder. My first pitch to him was way high, ball one. The second pitch went into the dirt. Ball two. Sometimes when you're tired you can throw hard but lose control and accuracy. I couldn't let that happen. The noise from the fans was now deafening, with Fisk in a hitter's count. I stepped to the rubber and stared down at my feet. I shook my arm out once, then did it again.

I threw my next pitch, and Fisk got a hold of it. The crowd roared in anticipation. But that afternoon the wind was going against balls to left field. Our left fielder, Roy White, was able to settle under it, in front of the wall, for the first out of the inning. Fred Lynn, their center fielder and the 1975 MVP, gave the next pitch a ride out to center field. Again, fans thought it might leave the park. Mickey Rivers, our fastest outfielder, was able to get under it. It wasn't pretty, but I was getting by. And I knew that's what I had to do. I wasn't going to be the untouchable pitcher I had been all season. But I had to find a way to get outs and dance out of trouble.

And that's what I did for the next several innings. I gave up a leadoff double in the third but didn't allow the runner to score. In the fourth, I got Rice, Yaz, and Fisk out in order. As he did the first time, Fisk smacked it high and deep, just high enough for Mickey to get to the edge of the warning track and catch it. I gave up a single in the fifth, but the runner never got past first. I was holding my own.

The problem was that Torrez was doing more than holding his own. He gave up just two hits in the first six innings. I'm not sure if he was out for revenge or just pitching a heckuva ball game, but we weren't scraping anything together at the plate. Nothing like we did during the season. We had faced him four times during the season and won three. One of those times we knocked him out of the game in the second inning. His stellar performance today made it all the more important that I keep things close.

Boston almost blew it open in the bottom of the sixth. And they would have if Lou Piniella didn't make the most unsung play in Yankees history. Rick Burleson began the inning with a double. Jerry Remy sacrificed him to third. Rice, who I had gotten out twice, came through like he so often did with a single, scoring Burleson. Rice moved to second on a Yaz groundout, then I intentionally walked Fisk. He was 0 for 2 against me on the day, but inches away from being 2 for 2 with two homers. So with runners on first and second, with two outs, Lynn stepped to the plate.

Now, our outfielders weren't regarded as the best fielders in baseball. Mickey, in center, could run. But Roy White, in left, and Lou, in right, weren't speed demons. But they *were* smart ballplayers. They were always paying attention and knew every facet of the game. Just because you're good enough to play in the majors doesn't mean you can't learn more. And they were always trying to stay a step ahead of what was happening on the field.

On that day, that meant closely eyeing how I was pitching. I hadn't started with my best stuff, and by late in the game I wasn't throwing as hard. When that happens, batters tend to get out in front of the ball and pull it more. Piniella and

White knew that, which is why they played such great defense all season. Nobody had to tell them to play a step this way, a step that way. They always seemed to shade over just the right amount. They weren't fast enough to chase down every ball, but they didn't have to most of the time because they were always in the right spot at the right time to catch them.

Lynn stepped to the plate; a hit from him could put the game out of reach. First pitch, ball one. Then a foul ball, strike one. Another foul ball, strike two. Finally, I was ahead on the count. The next pitch got away from me—ball two. I missed the plate again; ball three, full count. When he connected with my 3-2 slider, I thought for sure it would score two runs. He pulled it to the right-field corner, just shy of the wall. Even the fastest outfielder in the world had no business tracking that ball down. And Lou, our right fielder, was nowhere near the fastest outfielder on this or any other planet.

But Lou didn't have to go far. People thought he must have been psychic, because he was playing just a few steps away from where the ball was hit. Normally, he would be completely out of position. That was especially because Lynn never pulled the ball against me. But Lou knew today was different from any other day. So he played Lynn and he played me differently and put himself in the perfect spot. We used to joke with Lou that he was lucky at the plate. But nothing about that play in the field was lucky. Lou was a student of the game. He got there just in time to make a basket catch and end the inning. That play is nowhere near as famous as the one that came moments later. Still, it saved my ass. And our season.

As far as improbable heroics go, Lou was about to be one-upped. We were down 2–0, but our bats were too good to stay quiet forever. During the regular season, even when we trailed the Red Sox by fourteen games in the middle of the summer, it never dawned on us that we couldn't catch 'em. We felt the same way late in the playoff game. It never occurred to us that we wouldn't score and come back. The surprising part wasn't that we did it. It was how we did it.

———

"I was so damn shocked," Torrez would say later. We were all so damn shocked.

Boston had spent the afternoon hitting me around pretty good. But they only had two runs to show for it—it could have been more. And if it weren't for Lou's baseball smarts, it would've been more. But it was just two. And as easy as the early innings had been for Torrez—he had given up only two hits and had thrown close to seventy pitches so far—we knew we could score against him.

Graig Nettles, our third baseman, flew out to start the seventh inning. Not the start I had hoped for. Then Chris Chambliss, our first baseman, singled. So did Roy White. With Brian Doyle, our second baseman, due up to bat, Lemon made a surprising decision. He sent Jim Spencer to pinch-hit for Doyle. Spencer, a first baseman who mainly came off the bench for us, didn't hit for much average, but he had a lot of power. He took a huge cut, but it resulted in an easy flyout, putting two on with two outs for Bucky Dent.

Bucky was our number nine hitter. He was known best for being smooth in the field, and even though he was a tough out, he wasn't much of a threat to take an opposing pitcher deep. He had hit only four home runs all season and didn't hit for an especially high average, either. As the season went on, things only got worse for him at the plate. In our final nineteen games, he got just seven hits in fifty-four at-bats, a .130 average. Usually, in this situation, he'd be the obvious person to send in a pinch-hitter for. And Lemon wanted to do that. But he couldn't. He'd used Spencer to bat for Doyle, and Fred Stanley, our backup middle infielder, would have to replace Doyle at second. Willie Randolph, who usually started at second for us, was out with a hamstring injury. If Billy Martin had still been our manager, he probably would've saved Spencer to hit for Bucky. But Lemon didn't. And so because he had to use Stanley to replace Doyle in the field, he had to leave Bucky in.

But here's the thing about that season: On a team filled with stars, big personalities, and icons, somebody different stepped up every day. Some days it was me. Some days it was Reggie. Some days it was Munson. Or Willie. Or Goose. Or Lou would step up, like he did with that catch the previous inning. The stars weren't always the heroes. The heroes weren't always the stars. That day the hero was Bucky Dent.

As I sat in the dugout, I wasn't thinking about Bucky hitting a home run. Nobody was. That would be crazy. He hadn't hit one in a month and a half. I was thinking: If he can get a hit, someway somehow, we can get a run and then we're only down by one. One run in the final two innings is a whole lot easier than needing two to tie the game. I could go back out there, keep their bats quiet for another inning, and we could come back from one run down. So concentrate on getting one run.

Since spring training, Bucky had been hobbled by a ball he fouled off his shin. He was never quite right this season. It caused a blood clot, and later in the year he missed a month with a hamstring injury. Because he often had trouble with fastballs, fouling them off his leg, he started wearing a foam pad to protect that front, left leg. For whatever reason, maybe to try to break out of his slump, he didn't wear it that day. So naturally, when Torrez threw him an inside fastball, he fouled it off that same spot that had been killing him all year.

As soon as he did, he fell to the ground. He got up and hobbled around, trying to walk off the sting and regain his composure. He bent over and grabbed at the top of his foot, by the shin. He leaned back up and grabbed it again. He went down to one knee while Geno ran to check him out. Another reason he should've been pinch-hit for. And he could barely stand. As he got back up, he leaned on his bat for support. Geno sprayed him with something or other, patted him on the hammy, and sent him back out there. There was nothing else to do.

Strangely enough, all of this was the best thing that could have happened, for two reasons. First, Torrez was pitching well, but he was a pitcher who relied on rhythm. The delay, as Bucky gimped around, interrupted that. Sometimes in those moments, pitchers take some practice throws to keep loose. Torrez didn't. The second reason has to do with the keen eye of one of our other guys, Mickey Rivers. At some point during all of this, he saw a crack in the bat Bucky was using. Bucky was a long shot to get a hit to begin with, and nobody has a prayer with a broken bat.

Nobody saw it but Mickey, not even Bucky. "Homie," Mickey hollered from the dugout. "You got a busted bat there!"

He handed the bat boy a new bat. The bat boy ran it out to Bucky. He took it and strode back into the batter's box.

Following the delay, the crowd was quiet. Torrez stepped

back onto the mound and delivered a belt-high fastball, down the middle. Bucky connected. You didn't even have to watch the ball to know the sequence of events. You just had to listen to the crowd and watch Yaz out in left field. First, Yaz patted his glove a couple of times like he was going to catch it. Except as the day turned into early evening at Fenway, the wind had shifted. The same gusts that were keeping balls hit to the left in the park earlier in the game were now carrying them farther out. Yaz turned, getting ready to play it off the wall. Balls off the Green Monster can be held to singles.

From the bench, we were all hollering. "GO. GO. GO." A ball off the wall, even a single, would score that one run I was talking about. Maybe even two to tie it up, if it was a double. I knew what happened as I watched Yaz. He looked like he got punched in the stomach. His head tilted down. His body bent over. Fenway Park, and the raucous Boston fans, fell dead quiet as the ball disappeared behind the Green Monster for a home run. Save for the few Yankees fans who were there, and our entire bench, not a word was spoken in the stadium. Bucky never stopped running until he reached the dugout. We were all waiting outside, screaming and hollering. All of a sudden, to the disbelief of Yaz, Torrez, the fans, all of us, and the millions watching on television or listening on the radio, the scales tipped in our favor. Bucky Dent got a middle name in Beantown that moment for that improbable home run. Bucky F—ing Dent. Yankees 3, Red Sox 2.

Yankees announcer Phil Rizzuto explained the shock of an entire country: "I'm like a hen on a hot rock. I don't know whether to jump, or sit, or lay an egg."

The hit pretty much ended Torrez's day. He walked Mickey, up next, and was taken out of the game. Which was good news for Thurman, who had struck out three times in three at-bats against Torrez. Mickey stole second and Thurman doubled him home off Boston reliever Bob Stanley. A first insurance run. Yankees 4, Red Sox 2.

————

I took the mound to start the seventh inning and struck out Butch Hobson. I felt good. Then George Scott singled to right, and out came Lemon to take me out of the game. It was the first time I ever argued with Lem. I was pissed. I did not want to come out. He had Goose ready, and I understand that when you get a reliever ready, it's bad to let him warm up and then have him just sitting out in the bullpen. But I was mad that he got him ready. I may not have had my best stuff, but I was still going strong. I still had gas left in the tank. I wanted to, at the least, finish the seventh.

Yeah, I had just given up a hit, but it was a weak, twenty-hop ground ball between first and second. It wasn't like he slashed the ball or hit a line drive. That ball is an out most of the time. I could've kept going. I felt I should've kept going. And I was used to throwing deeper into games. I had only been taken out this early a handful of times all season.

"My job ain't finished," I told him. "Lem, I'm still strong. Leave me in."

Thurman joined us at the mound. He agreed with me and told Lemon I was still throwing the ball good enough. Lem shook his head. He said he had gotten Goose ready and that I'd done a hell of a job. Thurman slapped me on the back, and I begrudgingly walked to the dugout. Lem signaled for Goose. My day was done. Goose got out of the inning, but the game was far from over.

I watched the eighth inning from the clubhouse. I was physically drained and needed to ice down my arm. To begin the eighth inning, Reggie Jackson stepped to the plate. He had hit the ball hard earlier in the game but had nothing to show for it, 0 for 3. Say what you want about Reggie—and people, including Reggie himself, said plenty about him and his swagger—but there was only one thing to say about his ability as a batter: He was damn good at hitting the baseball. Despite everything that had happened with Reggie, Thurman, Billy, and George, I had so much respect for Reggie as a ballplayer. Not a big moment seemed to pass without him reminding people of how good he was. And that day, October 2, Mr. October, as he was called, clobbered a home run to dead center field, for what looked to be an insurance run. Yankees 5, Red Sox 2.

It turned out we needed that insurance. Goose was one of the finest and most consistent relief pitchers ever. But beyond being good, he was intimidating. He was not a man you wanted to see when you stepped into the opposing batter's box. At least, I wouldn't want to be 60 feet and 6 inches away from that arm, and that mug, trying to hit the ball. The only thing scarier than his blazing fastball was the nasty stare he gave a batter. He had wild hair. A big mustache. Nobody was more familiar with Goose than Boston. That season, even before the playoff game, he had thrown more innings against them than against any other team.

But no hitter owned Goose like Yaz did. Remy began the inning with a double. After Rice flew out, Yaz singled Remy home, kicking off a hit parade that would create an uproar at Fenway you could probably hear from New York. You could probably feel it in New York. Fisk followed Yaz with another single. Then Lynn singled. Goose got the next two guys, but the damage was done. The Red Sox had scored two runs. We went down quickly in the top of the ninth and needed three more outs to win. The margin was Reggie's solo shot. Yankees 5, Red Sox 4.

After Goose got the first out of the ninth, he walked Burleson. This game wouldn't end without more drama, and the tying run was on base. The Red Sox had been a great come-from-behind team all season. They just needed to do it one more time. Remy stepped to the plate next and roped a ball to Lou Piniella in right. At this point it was already past five o'clock. Around that time the shadows started to do funny things at Fenway. Lou was standing in the sun, with shade about twenty feet in front of him. Which makes it awfully hard to see the ball.

So when Remy hit that ball, nobody knew if Lou would catch it or not. Because Lou himself seemed to have no idea if he'd catch it or not. Usually you can tell by what the outfielder's doing, and how he's playing it, whether or not a ball will drop in. But because Lou had no idea where the ball was, he gave no indication. By the time he could see it again, it had landed a few feet in front of him and to his left. He had to make a herky-jerky stab at the ball just to prevent it from bouncing past him and rolling to the wall. But he didn't miss a beat and rifled the ball to third. Whatever you want to call it—luck because of the sun, Lou's savvy in not tipping his hand about not catching it, or headiness that he reacted so quickly and fired to third—it changed the outcome of the game. Because during all of this, Burleson, the runner on first base, didn't know whether he should be running to second—if it was a hit—or going back—if it was an out. Usually, he would've been on third after a single like that. Because of that indecision, and Lou's immediate throw to third, Burleson had to stay at second after it dropped in.

The next batter, Jim Rice, showed how crucial that was. He hit a towering fly ball, deep to right field. It didn't have a chance at going out, but if Burleson had been on third, he would've been able to tag up and score easily. That would've made the score 5–5 with Yaz coming up. Instead, Yaz came up with two outs, two on, and down 5–4.

Now Lem had one final decision. He could leave in Goose to face Yaz, who had gotten that big hit against him in the eighth. Or he could bring in Sparky for the last out. Sparky had been our closer in '77 and won the Cy Young. But when George brought in Goose in '78 and gave him the job, Sparky got diminished. Sparky, however, unlike Goose, was a lefty. It would make sense to bring him in to face Yaz, a lefty. Yaz owned Goose, but Sparky owned Yaz, holding him to a .147 batting average in their careers. Sparky was getting ready in the bullpen for just this moment. Lem didn't budge. He left in Goose.

I'm not sure it was the right decision. Maybe it was, maybe it wasn't. Sometimes the right decisions don't pay off and the wrong ones pan out. Who knows. But it worked. Yaz popped one high into the air down the left-field line. Nettles settled under it right by third base. He waited and closed his glove.

We jumped all over one another on the field, elated. Yet it was a somewhat subdued celebration because the game had taken so much out of us. The season had taken so much out of us. We were physically drained. It had taken every one of us in this traveling Bronx circus to get us to the playoffs. And tomorrow we had another performance.

2

WHO I AM AND WHERE I'M FROM

During spring training before the 1977 season, we went to play a game against Grambling. That's about a three-hour drive from where I grew up in Lafayette, Louisiana, and it was a natural opportunity for my folks, Roland and Grace, to see a game. My father and I had spoken on the phone, and I'd explained that I'd be able to spend some time with them. Spring games were very informal. It's not like there was a real dugout, just a fenced one, and after a few innings you could go hang out on the grounds and do what you wanted if you weren't playing.

"Want me to cook anything?" my father had asked. I could taste Louisiana home cooking on my tongue. We discussed the various menu options. But I knew what I wanted. I had a couple of rabbits that I had hunted stored away in the freezer, saved for rabbit stew. It was the perfect dish, and we could cook it up right by the field.

Sure enough, on game day my dad arrived at the ball field and set up his pot beneath a big oak tree. At some point George Steinbrenner rolled up to the field in his limo. I watched him having a conversation with Billy before a strange look came over his face. *Sniff*. He looked left, then right, trying to identify the source of the smell that caught his nose. *Sniff*.

Mr. Steinbrenner and I hadn't always gotten along so well at this point. Mainly, he had wanted to know why I hadn't done anything of note, while everyone around him kept telling him about the fireballing lefty from Louisiana who the Yankees would be crazy to trade away. Still, I went up to him and asked him if he'd like to meet my parents—the source of the aroma that I could tell he was thinking about. So I took him over and introduced them.

"Mr. and Mrs. Guidry, how do you do?" Steinbrenner said. "And what smells so good?"

"Well," my father said, "I'm cooking Ron his favorite, rabbit stew. We've got plenty, if you'd care to join us."

"I'd love to try some."

George proceeded to sit his ass down. He filled up his plate three times and nearly ate the whole damn pot. Boy, did he love it. If you've ever had traditional, fresh, Cajun rabbit stew, you'd probably do the same. Especially if it's a little cool out, it just hits the spot. Even if it's warm out. George thanked my parents for the meal and began walking away. Before he was out of earshot, he said to me, "Oh, by the way, if you don't bring this stew next year for spring training, don't bother coming."

And so I did just that every February for the rest of his life. I think he refused to eat any rabbit stew that wasn't Guidry rabbit stew. Even in his older years, after I had retired, even if he was in a meeting, once he saw me he'd get that look on his face he had the first time he smelled that aroma, and he'd chase everybody out of the meeting and say to me, "Got my stew?"

George wasn't the only person who got to know me and my roots through Cajun delicacies. Quickly it was the entire team. Whenever we'd play road games in Texas, my mom and dad would come to Arlington for the three or four games we'd play there. Daddy would always bring some food to cook for us. One time (in addition to the stew) he asked if I'd like anything else and I suggested he stop by the seafood place and get some frog legs for him and me to fry up. He got a couple dozen, and I didn't finish them all, so I brought the rest to the ballpark, planning to eat them after the game.

Well, I wound up having to share one with anybody who caught a whiff of them. They loved them. So the next time we went to Texas, Daddy invited a few of the guys to join us. All of a sudden, by 1978, he was hauling three hundred frog legs to Texas and practically the whole team was joining in.

Fast-forward to the 1990s, when I was going back to spring training as an instructor with the team. The great thing was that by a certain point, it felt like a reunion. Mickey Rivers, Graig Nettles, Goose Gossage, Willie Randolph, and others would all be back in Florida. So, of course, they eventually started saying, "Why don't you bring us down some of those frog legs for all of us to fry up next year?"

In time even the great Yogi Berra, who became my closest companion during spring trainings, grew to love them, even if in typical Yogi fashion he was a bit stubborn about it. I had brought a lot of them into the coaches' room one day for all of us to share and everybody started chowing down. Goose grabbed a handful and so forth, but not Yogi, in spite of everyone's encouragement.

"No, no, no," he kept saying.

We were supposed to eat at this place called the Rusty Pelican after the game, one of Yogi's favorites. I said, "Yogi, we're not going to the Rusty Pelican tonight if you refuse to try even one of my frog legs. You're going to eat a bologna sandwich in your hotel room in that case."

So he reached in. He nibbled a little bit. He nibbled a little more. He nibbled on the rest of it. He put the clean bone down. Sure enough, he stuck his hand back in the tray and grabbed as many as he could. Needless to say, we didn't have to go to the Rusty Pelican for dinner that night.

At the same time, you start to find out it's not just the coaches who want some. One day, Jorge Posada and Mariano Rivera came over. Both of 'em were giving me a look.

"We heard you were cooking frog legs for the coaches."

"We're coaches, you're players." I was teasing. So I cooked a dozen up for Mo. And a dozen for Jorge. It became an annual thing. Later with C.C. Sabathia, too.

What started with my bringing a small ice chest of food down to Florida every year had become so much I couldn't fit it all in one freezer. I always had to borrow space in Goose's freezer at the hotel. But the rabbit stew, can't let that out of my sight, or it'll all be gone. So the rabbit stew, that stays in mine.

———

I can't tell you about who I am without giving you a taste of where I'm from. Louisiana made me who I was, who I am, who I will always be. My two nicknames—Gator and Louisiana Lightning—are fitting because they pay tribute to my Cajun upbringing and my home state. It's a region of the country with a unique culture, historically and today: the cooking, the dialect, the terrain, the values. And it has never stopped being part of me. I have played home games at Yankee Stadium my entire career, but Lafayette has never stopped being my home.

———

My baseball career began in secrecy during the summer of 1958 in Lafayette. I was seven. I had never played. I didn't know yet that I loved the game. But I had taught myself how to throw, just throwing rocks by myself. Throwing a baseball isn't too different from throwing a good-sized rock.

The local team practiced at a playground on my street, about five blocks from my house. My mom wouldn't let me go farther than the next block. I kept telling myself, "One of these days, I'll just go find the field myself and not say anything." And that's exactly what I did. I told my mother I was going to my grandmother's house. She and Pop, my grandfather, lived in the house next to ours. Then I told my grandmother I was going to the grocery store at the end of the block. I walked all the way down the street, then cut back and kept walking until I found the playground.

I saw a bunch of kids fielding and a guy hitting balls to them. I kept walking until I passed all of them. I walked across the back of the field. My plan was to walk around them, then go back to where I'd started and head back home. All I wanted to do was check it out. But as I crossed the back of the outfield, the coach hit a ball to an outfielder, who missed it. The ball rolled to my feet.

Everyone screamed. "Throw the ball back!"

So I threw it back, past the kids in the field, past where the coach was standing. The coach started jogging toward me. I figured I had done something wrong, so I took off running away from him. He hollered after me to stop, then he asked me if I wanted to play ball. I told him who my dad was, and it turned out he knew my dad. The coach called him, they talked, and later I told Dad the story.

A couple of days later I was practicing. I didn't have a glove, so my dad bought me one. It cost fifteen dollars, which wasn't cheap back then. The only thing was, we didn't tell my mom. She didn't want me playing, because she thought it was dangerous. Her brother, my uncle, had gotten seriously hurt playing as a kid. So I slipped out for our practices and kept quiet about playing. I finally had to tell her on the day of the first game. She wasn't too happy.

———

I don't know how far back you'd have to go to find the first Guidrys in Louisiana, who came from Nova Scotia. To my knowledge, we'd always been here, in Louisiana, in Cajun country. Cajuns trace their roots back to France. French Catholics left for Canada in the early 1600s and, a little over a century later, some made their way to Louisiana. At some point, that included both my parents' families. And beginning on August 28, 1950, that included me.

To so many, Cajun culture means food. *Boudin. Gumbo. Jambalaya. Étouffée. Fried frog legs. Po' boys.* The foods I grew up on and learned how to cook are the same foods I eat and cook today. But I learned at an early age that Cajun culture isn't just about the food. It's about the people. It's about families—large families—and how they spend time together and depend on one another. Everything we knew, we taught one another.

My paternal grandfather, Gus, was one of eleven children. Like a lot of the families down here, ours was large and close-knit. Those eleven children had a lot of children, and a lot of them lived in Lake Arthur, a parish not far from us in Lafayette. We would have family gatherings at my great-grandfather's place, and there might be easily fifty people or more. Everybody brought food. They'd make a big jambalaya; there was always enough.

Most of my family were farmers. A lot of them farmed rice, some sugarcane. They didn't have a lot of money, and they lived off the land. They hunted. They trapped. And even though I didn't grow up on a farm, I learned to help when we visited. That's how it was. We all pitched in. My second cousin, also Ronald Guidry (we called him Joe) was three years my senior and taught me the ropes. When we were small, he showed me how to drive a tractor and how to work the combine, a machine that harvests the crops. You learn it because you have to. That was their livelihood and their way of life. And because you're part of the family, it's part of you too.

When Pop, my dad's dad, was young, he decided farming wasn't for him. He wanted to be a truck driver. When he was older, he became the dock foreman at the trucking line, running the shop. Dad worked on the railroad tracks, so he was gone every other day.

Pop and my grandmother lived next door in a small, two-bedroom house with a wooden frame and a little porch out front. Beneath the garage was a wooden swing where we'd sit and talk. In the backyard, family would come over and barbecue.

Pop taught me to hunt, which for us was not sport but a way of life. During the winter, during hunting season, we lived off the land, hunting duck, rabbit, dove, and quail. As a baseball player, I came back to hunting every off-season.

I was eight years old the first time Pop and I went duck hunting. We were at one of our relatives' places, out in a sunken blind in a rice field. It was early in the morning—some animals, like ducks and geese, he told me, are better to hunt in the morning. They go to feed and fly better for hunters. I had shot before, practicing in the woods, but never actually hunted. He gave me a crack-back barrel .410, a small-gauge shotgun. Small as it was, it was about as big as I was at that age.

Pop pointed into the misty air and told me to get ready. When the geese fly over, he said, I'd be able to hear them. "There's going to be a shadow in the fog," he said. "You pick one out and you shoot." Then we saw a bunch of silhouettes in the air. I fired. He fired.

I saw the bird I aimed at fall, but it wasn't dead. So I had to chase it for an extra twenty to thirty yards. By the time I got back to the blind, I noticed he had two in his hand. We shared a good laugh, because I only heard him fire once. Then, all of a sudden, we heard a couple more geese. He told me to take the one on the left and he would take the one on the right. Mine started to come right toward us. I fired, and it fell right by us in the blind. "At least I don't have to go chase it this time," I said.

It was a small moment that made both of us laugh. For us, hunting wasn't just for the practical purpose of feeding ourselves throughout the winter. In fact, you don't even have to shoot anything to have a meaningful experience. It's a shared experience. You go with your father or grandfather, your son or family members. You see a beautiful sunrise. You might see ten thousand ducks, or you might see just one. Who knows? A flock of ducks is pretty in and of itself. There's no 100 percent certainty you bag anything. But it's how memories are made, and for us, how a tradition gets passed on.

———————

Once I picked up hunting and baseball, the two activities neatly divided my year. Winter meant hunting. Summer meant baseball. If you had looked at me in my hunting gear, you might not have guessed I was one of the better players in baseball. Simply put, I was small. It's one of the reasons my mother was so nervous about me playing.

But I was always one of the better pitchers. The coaches would only pitch me against the other good teams in the league, and the league was small. This was the 1950s and 1960s, and the population of Lafayette was maybe forty thousand. There were maybe six to eight teams in each age group, and you played with the same kids every year.

For a long time, baseball was just something to look forward to in the summer. I mean, I loved watching baseball on television, and was a big Yankees fan even as a kid—they were the best team in baseball. The Mick, and Whitey Ford, Yogi Berra, and Roger Maris were my heroes. But I didn't think about playing baseball in college or the big leagues myself. Our parish didn't even have high school ball at the time, so I didn't play in high school.

I started playing American Legion when I was sixteen. I reached five feet eleven inches, the height I still am to this day, but I was rail thin. I might have weighed only 125 pounds. But the most important thing at this level was that I got first-rate coaching for the first time. I'd always been a good pitcher, but now I started to learn the intricacies of how to pitch.

I was one of the best players in the area, and that started to change my outlook. Baseball had always been just a game. But now it was starting to open doors that would've never been open to me. My dad never graduated from high school, and here my arm was about to take me to college. When I went to play baseball at the University of Louisiana Lafayette (then known as the University of Southwest Louisiana), for the first time I began to dream of something bigger. *Maybe,* I thought, *I've been looking at this all wrong.*

3

FORTY-SEVEN DAYS
IN HELL

I had driven down this highway many, many times before. I was on I-80 in Pennsylvania, not far from Harrisburg, in my brown Pontiac Grand Prix. There's a sign that says five miles to the turnoff for I-81. If you turn right there, you head north to Syracuse. If you turn left, you head south. I was supposed to go right, to Syracuse, where the Yankees had their Triple-A team. Turning left meant going back home to Lafayette, Louisiana.

Earlier that day the Yankees had split a doubleheader with the Kansas City Royals. Technically, I was still a New York Yankee, so I should say *we*. But it's difficult to feel like you're part of a team when you never play. For the forty-fifth and forty-sixth consecutive games, I sat on the bench, pulling splinters out of my ass. Why put me on the roster if I wasn't going to play?

When the second game wrapped up, I grabbed my jacket and headed back into the stadium. Our pitching coach, Bob Lemon, saw me and called me over. "Listen, I just have to tell you: When you get back in the clubhouse, they're going to send you down to Triple-A." Back to the minor leagues.

"Why?"

"You're not pitching," he said.

Well, shit. That wasn't up to me. It'd been forty-seven days since I last got put in a game. I didn't need to be a rocket scientist to know that I wasn't pitching. I wasn't even getting the chance to go out there and pitch badly. I just wasn't pitching at all.

There was no use in getting mad at Lemon. He had been a pitcher, a Hall of Famer. He knew what it was like. He was just doing his job. The guy who was managing, Billy Martin, he was the one who didn't want me around. He just didn't like me.

As I walked across the field, I decided, *I can't do this anymore.* I was about to turn twenty-six years old. My wife, Bonnie, was six months pregnant with our first child. I needed to provide for my family. If I had to do that by digging ditches, so be it—I was ready to get in line and start digging ditches. My family came first. If this was how they were going to treat me, there was no use in me staying. I would find something else to do.

I had made up my mind. I wasn't going to go back to Syracuse.

Packing up the car didn't take long. Bonnie and I had some clothes and a TV—that was it. I had proven everything I needed to prove in the minor leagues. I was going to turn left on Interstate 80—quit the New York Yankees and professional baseball.

———

The Yankees had taken me in the third round of the 1971 draft. I probably would've gone higher if I hadn't developed tendonitis in my arm while I was in college. It eventually caused me to drop out of school. But some things in baseball never change. A left-hander who can throw ninety-five-plus miles per hour was—and always will be—a valuable commodity.

The life of a professional ballplayer in the minors takes a lot of getting used to. You're leaving home, you're by yourself and need to make new friends. You need to find a place to stay, and you need to pay for everything yourself—you're not living at Mom and Dad's anymore. For most players, it's your first experience being on your own. And it's not as glamorous as some might imagine. We traveled on crappy school buses that broke down more often than not. It's a long way from the bright lights of the major leagues.

In those early years I did little out of the ordinary. Johnson City, Tennessee, was my first stop in 1971, as a rookie. The next year, 1972, I played Single-A ball in Fort Lauderdale, Florida. After that season Bonnie and I got married, so she traveled with me. She went where I went, which in 1973 meant Kinston, North Carolina. I had done nothing to convince the coaches I was major-league material. I struck out a lot of guys, but I walked a lot of guys too. I had only one pitch, really, my fastball. I could throw it by most people, but if I made a mistake, they'd kill me.

To compound matters, in those early years I was always on bad teams. No matter what organization you're in, it's hard to do well when everybody around you is struggling. My rookie year, we finished dead last in the league. The next two seasons we finished below .500. If you're on a good team, you can do more. On a bad team, you do less. It's a mind-set, and tough to break out of, as much mental as it is physical, especially as a pitcher. When you're not getting run support and the fielders behind you aren't making plays, it's difficult to be at your best. And more than that, there is the issue of who do you learn from to get better?

Bottom line—my first three years as a minor leaguer were mediocre. When I got to spring training in 1974, the Yankees asked me if I would entertain going into the bullpen as a relief pitcher. The organization had several talented young pitchers—including me—all ticketed for Double-A, too many for a starting rotation. Some guys might say no to becoming a reliever. Others, the team might not think would be able to transition to the bullpen. I said, "Sure, I'll give it a shot."

I hadn't distinguished myself as a starter. Maybe my ticket to the big leagues was as a reliever. If I could pitch nine innings, I certainly could pitch one inning. It seemed like a small decision at the time, but it would alter the entire path of my career—how I reached the majors, who I met, and what I learned. I didn't know it at the time, but I never would have become a star starting pitcher had I not toiled away in the bullpen.

But that 1974 season, beginning with change and optimism, became my worst. The team was awful. When you have a bad season and you're not winning, it's difficult to go out and pitch well. There's nothing inside that drives you, because no matter what you do, it's not going to make a difference. I turned twenty-four in Double-A with the West Haven Yankees and had a 5.26 earned run average. We finished with the worst record in the league. You can't make that stuff up.

After four years on crappy teams, I began to have negative thoughts run through my mind. *Maybe I'm not as good as I thought I was. Maybe I can't make a living doing this. Maybe I'm just not good enough.*

But it's easy to find hope. I read about guys I remembered striking out getting called up to the big leagues. Or seeing other pitchers get the call, and I'd say to myself, "Well, this guy isn't as good as I am, and he got a shot." Those things keep you going, plugging away.

The other good news was that for a pitcher, there are plenty of spots in the big club. If I was a catcher, I wasn't gonna take the job away from Thurman Munson. He wasn't going anywhere. If you were a first baseman in the minor leagues in 1985, you weren't going anywhere as long as the team had Don Mattingly. Or a shortstop in 2000 when the Yankees had Derek Jeter. But I was a pitcher, and I knew they had ten spots to fill. I just had to be good enough to be the tenth.

That hope was rewarded in 1975. Even though I had a bad year in Double-A in 1974, I was promoted to Triple-A in Syracuse. For the first time in my minor-league career, I was on a winning team. And as I discovered, when you're around other good players, it brings out the best in you.

But that wasn't the only change. First, there was our manager, Bobby Cox. Just a few years earlier, Coxy had been a major leaguer with the Yankees. A few years after I played for him, he would go on to manage in the big leagues for twenty-nine years, including twenty-five with the Atlanta Braves, winning five pennants and the 1995 World Series. It doesn't get much better than having Coxy as your Triple-A skipper.

Second, the players surrounding me were the best the organization had to offer. Some, like Scottie McGregor and Tippy Martinez, would go on to have long major-league careers. A few, like Tippy and Dave Pagan, had already been in the majors. In the majors you learn more in a week than you do in a month of minor-league ball. I hadn't been to the majors yet. But those guys passed along everything they'd learned—how to approach batters, work your pitches, and get outs. I was a sponge for information, trying to pick up everything I could, any little thing that could make the difference between becoming a major leaguer and washing out like the many thousands of minor leaguers who never crack the bigs.

"Pitch, don't throw" is a classic baseball adage. It was 1975 when I really learned how to *pitch*. I watched guys who threw ninety miles per hour get hitters out with ease. It's easy to just *throw* when you throw ninety-five miles per hour and can count on one hand all the people on this earth who can throw harder than you. But the hitters you go up against at this level are good too. That's why they're there. Pitching is about harnessing and fine-tuning what you're throwing, placing it on the corner. You can't be scared that the guy is gonna hit it, because he's going to. And you want him to swing at it but not have a great swing at it. You can't strike everyone out. But you can *try* to get everyone out. If you throw the ball in the right spot, most of the time, you'll get the right outcome. It's no different from anything else in life. You may be great at math, but you need to know what problem to solve. Sometimes savvy and know-how trump talent.

Coxy made me his closer in Triple-A. Now that I was surrounded by him and all these talented professionals, the minor leagues quickly changed from being a struggle to being easy for me. I was striking guys out, and when I wasn't, the defense was making plays behind me, just like they were supposed to. By the end of July, I was leading the league with fourteen saves and a 2.90 ERA, with seventy-six strikeouts in sixty-two innings. The league leader at the end of the year had fifteen saves. But that wasn't me.

That year Coxy was my biggest ally and advocate. When he saw the way I was pitching, he'd send reports to Yankees management, telling them, "Look, I got this kid—he does not belong here. You have to bring him up, okay?" They finally did, on Sunday, July 27. We were in Rochester at the time, and they rented me a car to drive back to Syracuse, where I grabbed some clothes and flew to New York. I had finally made the big leagues. I thought there was no going back.

That Sunday the Yankees had a doubleheader against the Red Sox. I arrived at Shea Stadium during game one. In 1975, Yankee Stadium was in the middle of a two-year renovation, so we split time at Shea, in Queens, with the Mets. I got to the ballpark and was quickly ushered into the locker room, where our clubhouse guy, Pete Sheehy, told me to get my uniform and meet the manager, Bill Virdon, who sent me down to the bullpen.

Then I got to the bullpen. I didn't know the guys. But I knew of them: Sparky Lyle, Dick Tidrow—two of the best relievers in all of baseball. And within a couple of minutes they were talking to me, figuring out what to call me.

"What do they have a lot of in Louisiana?" Tidrow asked.

"Well, we got a lot of snakes, frogs. We got a lot of rain. We got a lot of alligators . . ."

I looked down. Lo and behold, my shoelaces were on fire. Sparky had lit me up. *Welcome to the big leagues.*

Then Dick looked at me again. "We like you," he said. "We won't call you Alligator. We'll call you Gator for short." The nickname stuck. I was Gator for the rest of my career.

That same day, in the second half of our doubleheader, I got into my first game, facing the heart of the Boston Red Sox order, which included three future Hall of Famers: Jim Rice,

Carlton Fisk, and Carl Yastrzemski. I got Rice and Yaz out. Rice, who finished third in the MVP voting that year, was my first major-league strikeout. I finished the game without allowing a run in two innings.

But it didn't matter. That season, 1975, I pitched my first nine games out of the bullpen. And we didn't win any of them. Every single game I got into, we lost. I pitched just fine—I had a 1.74 ERA in those nine appearances. But the team wasn't going to put me in for an important situation. Heck, they never trusted me with a gigantic lead, only when we were getting blown out. I made the first start of my career in late September, again against the Red Sox. We were long out of the pennant race by then, and injuries to our staff had put me out there. In five and two-thirds innings—as many innings as I had thrown in the last month—I gave up four runs, while a Louisiana-style downpour drenched Shea Stadium.

The big thing going on was that in my first week with the team, owner George Steinbrenner sacked manager Bill Virdon. The Yankees had gone 89–73 in 1974, and we were supposed to be competing for the pennant in '75. Steinbrenner had shelled out $3.75 million for Catfish Hunter, and with that kind of spending he expected to win the title. Virdon was fired with a 53–51 record, because that just wasn't cutting it. We had lost eighteen of our last twenty-nine games. Virdon's replacement: Billy Martin.

Billy Martin brought a lot of credibility to the job. He brought the street cred of the legendary Yankees teams, having won four World Series as a player, in 1951, 1952, 1953, and 1956. He brought managerial success, having won more games than he lost in three stops: Minnesota, Detroit, and Texas. He also brought a lot of baggage. There's a reason the man had been sacked from three manager jobs in less than a decade. As a player, he was a scrappy fighter. He was fired in Minnesota because he beat the tar out of one of his players outside a bar. In Detroit he was let go after a suspension for telling his pitchers to throw spitballs. He was fired from his job in Texas just a few weeks before we hired him.

Of all the things that have been said about Billy Martin, the one that mattered to me was that he did not like rookies. And I was an inexperienced player. This didn't just mean he didn't pitch me much. He didn't even talk to me much.

So the next year, when I arrived at spring training at our complex in Fort Lauderdale, it felt like I was on a different team. This was Billy's first full season as manager. The Yankees had made a bunch of big moves during the off-season, so even the guys in the clubhouse were different. We traded starting pitcher Doc Medich to the Pirates, getting back a massive haul: Dock Ellis, Willie Randolph, and Ken Brett. We also traded away Bobby Bonds (who at the time had an eleven-year-old son named Barry, who you also might've heard of) for Mickey Rivers and Ed Figueroa.

I did not pitch well in spring training. The thing is, I never had good spring trainings in my career, because I didn't throw during the off-season. When I threw that last pitch in September, I didn't throw another baseball until that first day of camp. Not because I was lazy. I consciously rested my body all winter. Every year I went home to Louisiana during the off-season with Bonnie and my kids. I lived in New York during the season, but Louisiana was my home. I saw family and friends and went hunting, bringing back ducks, rabbits, quails.

And even though my off-season approach meant I came

back rusty, I knew it was best for me. Spring training games don't count; all that mattered was that I was ready when the season actually started in April. The worst thing would be if I tried to throw during the winter and tired my arm out for the season. My arm needed to rest.

So when I got to spring training, I had to take my time to build up my strength. I would start slowly, throwing only fast-balls at first. And I'd get lit up a lot because all I was throwing was fastballs. My slider wouldn't work if my fastball wasn't where it was supposed to be, so it wasn't worth throwing early on. Besides, my slider wasn't very good at the time.

The purpose of spring training is to get ready for the season. It's not part of the season itself, so that's how I looked at it: I'm gonna take my time. But that's not how Billy saw it. "You're getting hit. Why?" Well, heck, I saw he wasn't saying anything to the veteran pitchers who were getting lit up during the exhibitions. Catfish was getting hit. Sparky was getting hit. Everybody on the staff was getting hit. But they were all experienced guys. Billy wasn't gonna say shit to them. But I was a rookie, so he decided to pelt me because he didn't think I was doing my job. That's just the way it was.

At the end of spring training I had just boarded the team bus to head north. Billy called me off into the parking lot. He explained that because of the trades we had made, especially getting Ken Brett, there wasn't a spot on the roster for me. Brett was a veteran, so he was out of options—he couldn't be sent back down to the minor leagues. I had options. So I was getting sent back down to Triple-A.

I understood. I wasn't too upset. So I went down from Fort Lauderdale to Hollywood, Florida, where the Triple-A team was practicing. Coxy was already waiting for me; he knew what was going on. "Okay, fine," he said. "They're going to give Brett a shot, and if he doesn't work out, you'll be called right back up there."

Triple-A had been easy for me the year before. Now it was a joke. All of the knowledge that I had gained in the last two-plus months with the Yankees, as well as two more months in spring training with them, made it all too easy. By the middle of May I was mowing down batters left and right, and the Yankees decided Ken wasn't working out and traded him away. They called me back up on May 20. Again I went through the drill of getting my stuff and going back to New York. I hoped this would be the final time.

The day I was called up, Billy put me in a game. Most of the time that would be welcome news to me. But I had just pitched a few nights in a row in the minor leagues, and Coxy had sent a report saying I should have a couple days off. Of course, Billy ignored that and threw me into a game right off the bus. I just didn't have very much. He was sending me out to slaughter. I recorded one out and gave up four runs.

Billy had gotten Coxy's report. But he was testing me, because he didn't want me there; he was setting me up for failure. I don't know exactly why. Maybe because I was a rookie and he wanted a more experienced guy. But it was clear he didn't like me.

So began my stint in hell. For forty-six games and a total of forty-seven days, I parked my ass in the bullpen and never pitched. In 1975 at least I was being given the chance to pitch when we were getting blown out. Now I wasn't even getting that opportunity. The calendar flipped from May to June to July, and I didn't pitch in a single baseball game.

It's not like Billy forgot about me. In the fifth inning the phone in the bullpen would ring. "Okay, get Guidry up, and get Tidrow up." And we'd get ready. I'd get my arm loose and start throwing. The phone would ring again. Tidrow was going in the game. The next time there were problems, I got up again. Somebody else went in.

The ironic thing was that every time there were trade rumors, my name was involved. It seemed like everyone wanted me except the New York Yankees. But the weird thing was, the Yankees didn't want to let me go. In June, smack-dab in the middle of my bullpen-prison sentence, the Yankees traded Tippy Martinez, Scottie McGregor, Dave Pagan, and a couple of other guys in a big deal with the Orioles. Now, Tippy went on to be a great reliever in Baltimore, but the Orioles didn't want Tippy—they wanted me. The trade only went through because they accepted Tippy when our general manager, Gabe Paul, my biggest advocate in the front office, refused to give me up.

At the time I didn't know exactly what was going on in the front office. But here's what you had at play: Billy was bitching and moaning because I wasn't doing my job. So, of course, when the field manager is pissed off, Mr. Steinbrenner gets upset. He was paying a player who was not living up to expectations. So George wanted me gone. Meanwhile, our general manager refused to trade me. This would happen again the following spring. And all the while, guess what? I wasn't pitching.

I didn't look at it like I was getting cheated. I looked at it more like it was a test of my character. My teammates were a crutch. They had troubles too, whether personal or professional. It wasn't just me. But everybody else was in a good frame of mind, thankful to be there playing the game. Looking at them, knowing everybody was dealing with their own problems and holding their heads up, gave me some strength. That's what I had to do. I had to do as good a job as I could, and if that wasn't good enough, it wasn't meant for me to be here.

But the hardest thing during this entire time was feeling invisible. I wasn't a "name guy." The guys who I hung around with in the bullpen accepted me for who I was, but I didn't get the nod from anyone else because I wasn't doing a job yet. I didn't have a function. It's not like I was doing the job badly, I just wasn't playing at all.

Off the field, I didn't have a routine yet either. I hadn't earned the right to act in a certain way that might attract attention because I hadn't paid my dues. It's not like I could jump right into the shenanigans and do what everyone else was doing. Young guys like me and Willie Randolph, who was playing his first full season in 1976, didn't do anything to step out of line. We stayed on the straight and narrow. On the other hand, you'd see high-priced guys like Catfish Hunter parade through the locker room, go through his mail, sign some autographs for fans, drink some coffee, shoot the shit with Munson, and hash things out. It was their routine.

At the core, there are two types of acceptance in the clubhouse: for the player you are and for the person you are. But you can't show the person you are without showing the player you are. And l didn't have the opportunity to show the player I could be because I wasn't playing. You can have a great personality, but if you're not playing, you're not helping the team. Guys don't look at you the same way.

Naturally, you grow closest with people who do the same job as you. I was closer with the guys who pitched than I was with the everyday players. That didn't mean I couldn't be great friends with them, but I had more to talk about with the other pitchers. The hitters didn't want to get into the nitty-gritty about how to set hitters up, they just wanted to know how to hit the ball. I was going to learn more from talking to the pitchers.

When I sat down in the bullpen, I had Sparky Lyle on one side and Tidrow on the other. These are two great pitching minds, and two people who became great friends. Sparky didn't say very much. Tidrow would talk to me more. He would tell me how to set up hitters and attack them. He would make me watch other pitchers who were left-handed and threw the ball hard like I did. I would watch those lefties when they were pitching against us. Vida Blue, a star pitcher on Oakland at the time, was one of them. Vida threw hard and he had a great breaking ball. I looked at what he was doing, and I could see why he was so successful. That was the whole thing for me: developing a different pitch to go along with my fastball. I threw hard, but I just didn't have that something else. That's where Sparky came in.

During this miserable period when I wasn't pitching, Sparky started to work with me on throwing a slider. Like me, he was a lefty, and we had similar mechanics. He was also one of the best relievers in the game. We talked about how to throw a slider it, how to use it, and when to use it. When Billy inevitably called the bullpen and told me to get up and throw, Sparky made me work with it a little bit more each time. And I was finally starting to get it.

I just didn't have the chance to show it.

———

Turn right: Triple-A. Turn left: home. After those forty-seven days without getting a chance to pitch, being sent back down to the minors, packing up the car—that's when I broke down. I was on I-80, five miles away from the turnoff, from the fork in the road. Five minutes from giving up on baseball.

"I can do the job, but I'm never going to get a fair shake. This guy doesn't trust me," I told Bonnie, referring to Billy Martin. As much as I'd tried to stay positive, I was sick of the shit Billy was shoveling. Going back to Triple-A would be a total mismatch, given everything I'd learned from Tidrow over the last month and a half about how to pitch. More important, now I had the slider I developed with Sparky. I felt like I had everything I needed to succeed in the majors. But I couldn't get into a game.

"If I go back to Syracuse, I might be there for one week and get called right back up," I told her. "You might have to pack up the car and come back to New York to meet me."

"Look, if it's worth one more try that might make the difference, I'm willing to do it," Bonnie told me. "If you quit and you go home, it will be the first time I've ever known you to quit something before you realized whether or not you were good enough to do it."

"Okay, I'll give it one more shot," I said. "But if it doesn't work, that's it."

"Okay, fine," she said.

And as quick as that, I saw the intersection and went right.

4

"GET YOUR ASS OFF MY MOUND"

For the sixth time in my first seven starts in '77, I had taken the New York Yankees into the ninth inning with a lead. And for the sixth time, I stood on that mound and silently seethed at the familiar sight of Billy sauntering from the dugout in his bowlegged duck walk to take me out.

It was June 16, 1977. We led the Royals 7–0. And Billy's routine was quickly growing old. It made my blood boil. Back then, pitchers finished games—we didn't automatically hand the ball off. Not like today. It made me want to take a swing at Billy, the way Billy took a swing at so many people since he first picked up a glove. As a player and as a manager, Billy Martin was a fighter. Scrappy, like a bantam rooster, quick to come at you. He never felt it was his job to be chummy with his players. And he sure as heck had never been chummy with me. Since the first day I put on a Yankees uniform, he had been at me, alternately pushing and ignoring me. He insulted me, demeaned me. And even now that I was in the rotation, pitching well, he didn't trust me.

He kept coming out during the ninth inning, when I was a couple of outs away from ending the game. Every time the same thing happened: someone would get on base, and he would immediately hop out of the dugout. As he reached the top step, he'd signal with one arm or the other. *Give me the righty. Give me the lefty.* Either way, my day was done. By the time he had reached the mound, all he would say was "Good job," and I was out of the game. It was too late to say shit. The decision had already been made. The reliever was already jogging in from the bullpen. I was in the dugout by the time he reached the infield.

Every time it happened, I got more and more fed up. This was about more than simply being taken out of a ball game. I was pissed because in essence what Billy was saying was, he didn't trust me. Didn't matter how well I was pitching. But doing something about it wasn't so easy. Was I supposed to *challenge* him? The great Billy Martin? Was that the smart move for a twenty-seven-year-old pitcher who, at that moment, could've very well been home riding a tractor in Louisiana? All I knew was that while I respected Billy as a manager, I wasn't afraid of him.

———

After I decided not to pack my bags and head home the summer of 1976, I didn't have to wait long to get called back up. A month later, in early August, I became a New York Yankee again. After seventy-eight days—forty-seven riding the pine, thirty-one in the minors—I was back in the show. Of course, Billy still trusted me about as far as he could spit. For example, I was trotted out in the middle innings of a game we were already losing 4–0 to the Orioles. I gave up three runs in three innings and we lost. I got back in the next day—we were losing badly again—and this time threw two shutout innings. Then I spent two weeks on the bench.

My next appearance, August 22 against the Angels, brought me face-to-face with the Boss. We were down 4–0 with one out in the seventh, and Billy brought me in to replace Catfish Hunter, who'd left runners on first and third. Here in a nutshell is the frustration of pitching: You can sometimes throw great pitches, get weak contact from the hitter, and yet it's a hit. The opposite is equally tough on hitters. They can whack the bejesus out of the ball but hit it right at a fielder for an out. Today a bunch of dinks and dunks found some open space. Eight outs later, I had given up five hits. I let Cat's two runners score in the seventh and allowed two more to cross home in the ninth. We scored eight runs in the bottom of the ninth, then lost in extra innings. It was a crushing loss.

But losing the game wasn't as demoralizing as what happened next. My brief career as a Yankee had hardly been noteworthy to this point. I felt invisible and hardly used. But George didn't buy the team to sit back and watch. He put himself in the thick of it. He wasn't out to make friends, either. He was out to win. Steinbrenner thought he knew everything, and he wanted to know why the left-handed pitcher who people kept telling him not to trade had a dismal 10.12 ERA on the season. In four relief appearances that year I had allowed nine runs. The two runs I allowed in two and two-thirds innings actually *lowered* my ERA. So he called me into his office. The king wanted an audience. He wanted to lash out at the little-used, twenty-fifth guy on the roster.

"When," he snapped, "are you gonna start pitching?"

I didn't know what I was supposed to say to that. The fact was, Billy didn't want to pitch me. He only stuck me in when it didn't matter. I had proven myself in Triple-A. Still, the organization sent me up and down, jerked me left and right.

But some in the front office had a feeling I had something, that I could be something. There was a reason other teams were desperate to trade for me. With everything I had learned from Sparky Lyle and Dick Tidrow, the pitching coaches saw in me the makings of a major-league pitcher, a starter. Except I was only being tossed into blowouts. I never faced pressure situations against other lefties, when I could be most effective.

"By our reports," Steinbrenner went on, "you should be striking out every batter you face."

That was George Steinbrenner in a nutshell. His irascibility, his expectations, his outlook, how he confronted people. I was supposed to strike out every batter I faced. That is the world George lived in. I told him that was impossible, and I was never put in the right situations. They warmed me up almost every game and never used me. Then, when they did, I had warmed up in every game all week and wasn't fresh. I was being treated like clubhouse furniture and was getting blamed when I didn't perform.

When I told him that, he said, "That doesn't excuse how you pitched." He wouldn't hesitate to send me back to Syracuse, he snapped. If George was trying to get under my skin, he was succeeding. Then, before stomping out of the room, he said disparagingly, "Guidry, you'll never be able to pitch in this league."

———

Things didn't get much better for me as the '77 season kicked off. The team was already unhappy with me because I refused to go to Venezuela to play winter ball, as they suggested. Bonnie was due, and we'd had a bad experience in Venezuela the previous year. Then I sucked again during spring training. I had never worried about the results in spring training before, but Billy and the front office did. And my results weren't pretty. In six games I had a 10.24 ERA. Then I was hurt and missed some starts. When I came back, I wasn't yet at full strength and got smacked around pretty good. If there was one thing in the entire world George and Billy could agree on, it was that I stunk. And like George, Billy told you exactly how he felt.

That, for better or for worse, was just Billy. What you saw is what you got with him. For a long while I didn't like it, but he never shied from telling me his opinions. And until I proved myself to him, nothing would change. But he wouldn't lie to you. He'd say it to your face. He'd tell it to the press. He'd say it in the locker room. It might have been his biggest problem as a manager—that he was so blunt, straightforward, and steadfast in what he believed.

But that's how Billy had defined himself as a player. And he had become a Yankees legend. A second baseman on the great Yankees teams in the 1950s, he wasn't the guy who hit for power. But he solidified his status in other ways. There were the actual things he did on the field, like the incredible performance that made him MVP of the 1953 World Series. But with Billy, it was always more about attitude. He had a feistiness that resonated with fans in the Bronx. He wasn't particularly big, strong, or fast. The Yankees baseball cap never seemed to fit quite right on him, like his head was too big in the front and too narrow at the back. But he wasn't about fitting in, he was about playing baseball, grinding, fighting, and winning.

And he had the same sort of attitude as a manager. He was a winner, although it was never easy or pretty. In Minnesota, Detroit, and Texas, before George hired him, he had been a winner. But he also left a bitter taste in people's mouths because he was rough around the edges. He would get into fights. He would drink. He never looked quite healthy, though it was tough to tell if that was just because he worked himself to the bone. There was no questioning his work ethic. George must have known all of this when he hired him. As much as they fought, it was that competitive spirit that made them kindred souls.

That was the sort of attitude that led Billy to lay it all out on the line with people. For me, as someone who was struggling, that was tough. "If there's anybody in this league you can get out, lemme know," Billy snarled at one point. "I'll let you pitch to him."

————

In April of '77 two things—both completely out of my control—turned everything around. The first happened in a game I was watching from the bench. Our fourth game of the year, we opened a series in Kansas City. We came in having lost two straight, and even though it was only April, our results were starting to get the team on edge. This was a team that everybody—fans, the media, George, Billy, and the guys in the clubhouse—expected to win it all. We had reached the World Series in 1976. The Reds steamrolled us in a four-game sweep. But honestly, we were just happy to be there. Not only was it the first trip for the Yankees to the World Series since George bought the team in 1973, it was the first time we'd made it since the days of Mickey Mantle and Whitey Ford in 1964.

A 1-2 start means nothing over the course of a baseball season. Except in New York, with the attendant personalities. In the off-season, we had added Reggie Jackson, the

Playing for the University of
Southwestern Louisiana, 1971.
*(Edith Garland Dupré Library,
University of Louisiana at Lafayette)*

Playing Triple-A ball at
Syracuse in 1975.
*(© Jeffrey W. Morey,
Syracuse, NY/Syracuse Chiefs)*

Bonnie and me on
our wedding day,
September 23, 1972.
(Courtesy of the author)

The Yankees starting pitching staff in 1977: Ed Figueroa, Mike Torrez, Catfish Hunter, and me.
(Courtesy of the author)

Relaxing before a game.
(Harry Harris/ Associated Press)

Eating ribs and icing my arm after a game.
(Associated Press)

With Manager
Billy Martin.
(Associated Press)

In the dugout
with reliever
Goose Gossage.
(Associated Press)

With Yankees third
baseman Graig Nettles.
(Associated Press)

Being congratulated by the team after winning Game 4 of the 1977 World Series against the Dodgers. *(Associated Press)*

Being congratulated by Thurman Munson and Chris Chambliss after striking out eighteen batters in a game against the California Angels in 1978. *(Richard Drew/Associated Press)*

With Thurman Munson in Game 3 of the World Series against the Dodgers in 1978. *(Heinz Kluetmeier/Getty Images)*

With Reggie Jackson, after beating the Los Angeles Dodgers in the sixth and final game of the 1978 World Series. *(Bettmann/Getty Images)*

Pitching off the mound: At 5'11", I needed perfect mechanics to generate that 95 mph fastball. *(Michael Zagaris/Getty Images)*

A time-lapse sequence of my pitching motion. *(Focus on Sport/Getty Images)*

Hunting for ducks in
the Louisiana bayou.
(Courtesy of the author)

With my wife, Bonnie.
(New York Daily News)

power-hitting star outfielder, to the mix. If a team could win the World Series based on magazine covers, you'd have thought that with signing Reggie, we had a lock on the title. But that's not how baseball is played. We got a good hitter, without question. But with his personality, bringing him on board was like pouring gasoline on an already combustible situation. Even the smallest spark could set things off. Trade rumors, including rumors involving me, swirled. Folks questioned Billy's competence. George and Billy fought each other fiercely in public—and in private. And fans and the media began to openly wonder if George's micromanagement was the root of the problems. As the *New York Times* put it that April: "It would be the ultimate in irony in the wacky world of the Yankees if the goose that laid the golden egg stepped on the egg and splattered it."

It was with these tensions in the background that we approached the game in Kansas City. It might've been only the fourth game of a 162-game season, but it felt far bigger. And beyond all the hoopla around us, the Royals weren't just any other team. They were our expected competition in the American League, the team we beat in last year's playoffs. They had some great ballplayers in George Brett, Hal McRae, Al Cowens. It was as much of a litmus test of how good we were as you could imagine so early in the season. You could sense the excitement in Kansas City and the anxiety in our dugout. Billy rejiggered the lineup before the game, moving Jim Wynn up to the cleanup spot. That sent Reggie from fifth to sixth in the batting order, a constant source of anger for George, who wanted his star slugger batting fourth. Royals fans packed the stadium; they were excited because their team had started the season 3-0. I read afterward that one fan dressed as George handed out fake dollar bills to the Kansas City fans. April baseball games don't get more intense.

That game was tied 4–4 after five innings. For another seven innings, neither team scored. Dock Ellis had started the game for us and threw six innings. Then Sparky came in in relief and went five without allowing a run. And Tidrow got through the twelfth. Now, Tidrow was one of the two most important guys in my development as a pitcher. The previous season, he had taught me how to attack hitters and explained the strategy behind it. At the same time, he supported me psychologically while I was getting shit from Billy and George. He and Gabe Paul, our general manager, had my back.

Before Billy put Tidrow in the game, he had called the phone in the bullpen. He asked me if I was ready. I said yes. Then Sparky got on the phone to talk to Billy and had a confused look on his face. He turned to Tidrow, instead of me. "You're in the game." Dick got the Royals 1-2-3.

But Dick was a righty, and lefties hit him much harder than righties. Batters typically struggle more against same-handed pitchers. And in the thirteenth, he had to face the top of the Kansas City order, which featured two lefties. George Brett came on with one out and a runner on second. He was given an intentional walk. McRae flew out, to make it two outs, before another lefty power hitter, John Mayberry, came to the plate. I was ready in case Billy called. As a lefty, I was perfect for the spot. Especially with the slider I had developed thanks to Sparky. I knew I could be tough against lefty batters. Mayberry hit .226 against lefties and .266 against righties in his career. But Billy didn't call me in, and Mayberry smacked one of Tidrow's pitches off the wall, and that was the game.

When we went into the clubhouse after the game, the reporters were all over Billy. "Why did you leave Tidrow in? Why are you warming Guidry up if you're not going to use him in that situation?" I was wondering the same thing myself. A lot of us were. Nothing against Dick, it was just that the numbers said I was the better choice. But Billy hated all that crap. And he hated people questioning him or second-guessing him. He tried to brush off the reporters. Dick's a veteran, he said. Guidry doesn't have the experience.

Then a reporter asked him the question that had been on my mind for a couple of years now. "How in the hell is he going to get that experience if you never bring him in?"

The second night in Kansas City the same scenario played out. We were tied 3–3 in the seventh after our starter that day, Ed Figueroa, gave up back-to-back doubles, and the top of their lineup was coming up. Billy looked to his pen. On other days, Sparky would've been the obvious choice. But he had thrown five innings the day before so he wasn't available. The phone rang in the bullpen, and I was in.

I would've loved to be sitting next to Billy at that moment, because I'm sure he was furious he had to put me in. But with Sparky unavailable, Tidrow having pitched the prior day, and Billy having faced all those haranguing questions from the media, he didn't have much of a choice. But for Billy, it was a win-win. If I blew it, he was vindicated. If I pitched well, the Yankees would win.

In any event, I was thrilled to be in the game. This wasn't just my first game of the season—it was the first time I was pitching in a game that mattered. And I hadn't pitched in the '76 playoffs. It was a pivotal game and a chance to prove myself. What I didn't like was that George Brett was the first guy I had to face, with a man on second base.

George Brett is one of the greatest hitters to play the game. He batted over .300 in his career and hit more than three hundred homers. He hit for power and average. He hit a huge home run in the playoffs against us the previous year, tying game five at 6 apiece. Forget lefty on lefty, this guy could hit anybody.

And he hit me, roping a single right up the middle. *Damn.* Except Mickey Rivers, our fastest outfielder, was playing center. And Royals Stadium had turf in the outfield, so the ball skidded fast. On grass, especially when it's wet, the ball can slow down so that it takes a while for the outfielder to get to it. In Kansas City it zipped right to Mickey, who fired home and nailed the runner from second base at the plate. *Phew.* Then, with two outs, I walked McRae to face Mayberry, the other lefty. And I struck him out. I pitched two more scoreless innings after that without allowing a hit, and we scored in both the eighth and ninth to win 5–3. It was my first major-league win.

You know what Billy told the reporters after the game? "I planned that all along. I wanted to bring Guidry along slowly." Yeah, sure. Like I said, it was a win-win for Billy.

———

My second break came at the end of April. I was getting into games sporadically but still wasn't one of the main guys. And then those trade rumors that had been swirling around the clubhouse finally came to fruition. Except it wasn't what so many people expected—the deal didn't involve me. That was Gabe Paul's influence. He had seen the reports about my stuff in the minors and knew I could be good. He also had a hunch that if other teams wanted me, there was a reason. So we ended up trading pitcher Dock Ellis, a guy Billy and George disagreed about. Billy saw Dock as an important part of his rotation. George saw a pitcher who had called him out in the press for underpaying him. These days, Ellis is most famous for saying he was on LSD during the no-hitter he threw with the Pirates in 1970. In any event, he was gone, traded to Oakland, and in return we got Mike Torrez.

The Yankees traded for Torrez on Wednesday, April 27. He was expected to start that Friday, April 29. Should have been no problem. But instead of flying straight to New York, Torrez flew home to Montreal first to tend to a family health issue. Remember, this was before everybody could communicate so easily and send a quick text message or e-mail to clarify what was going on. Not everything was made clear to the team, and Torrez didn't know he was slated to start. And the afternoon of the game, Billy had no starting pitcher. He couldn't use Tidrow or Sparky because they were his setup guys in the bullpen, and he couldn't turn to some of the other relievers because they had pitched prior days. So after I got to the ballpark, as I was leaving the clubhouse to go to the bullpen, Billy called me over. Our interaction was brief and to the point.

"You're going tonight."

"All right," I said. And with that I was the starting pitcher.

Nobody expected much of me. I had been working as a reliever, preparing to take the ball at a moment's notice. I had started only once in the big leagues, in 1975, and that was in a meaningless game in September, against the Red Sox, where I gave up four runs in five and one-third innings. Not impressive. But not dreadful, either. Anyway, it felt like a lifetime ago. And by that day I was a totally different pitcher, with everything I'd learned from Tidrow and the slider I worked on with Sparky. But those things had made me a viable reliever. Could I prove myself as a starter? I wasn't so sure. Nobody expected me to blow hitters away. Billy told me he wanted me to make it through five innings; the bullpen could go the rest of the way. But even he understood that it's no small thing to learn you're the starting pitcher right before the first pitch.

An hour later I stood on the rubber at Yankee Stadium against the Seattle Mariners, 60 feet 6 inches from home plate. I struck out their leadoff man, but then things started unraveling quickly. Craig Reynolds singled. Steve Braun walked. Juan Bernhardt singled. Bases loaded, one out. This could've gone one of two ways. I could've given Billy every reason to never call my name again. Or I could prove myself by working my way out of it.

First came Bill Stein, who I struck out. That was an especially big deal, because with the bases loaded, there are a lot of ways to score a run. Fanning him meant it didn't matter how I got the next guy, Danny Meyer. An out, any out, would end the inning.

Meyer was a lefty, which I liked, but he had dangerous power. In '77 he hit twenty-two homers with 90 RBI. I worked the count to 2-2. The slider I threw next is what baseball folks like to call a cement mixer—basically, the ball spins but doesn't move. Usually it's hit a far ways off. Meyer connected . . . but it went foul. I wasn't about to make the same mistake again. Next I threw a good slider. Strike three.

As rattled as I was in the middle of the inning, I had proved to Billy—and to myself—that I could work my way through a jam. I struck out the first two guys in the second inning as well. The first five outs were all Ks. By the time Billy pulled me for Sparky with one out in the ninth, I had allowed just seven hits and no runs, and won 3–0.

———

I may have sent a message with that start, but it didn't get results immediately. Even though I was lights out that day, once Torrez arrived we had our five starters. I went eight games over nearly two weeks without setting foot on the mound again, before I got another relief appearance. Then, on May 17, Billy needed me to start again. Catfish had gotten hit around the last time he was out and spoke up about a sore shoulder that had been bothering him.

For eight innings in that start, the A's couldn't touch me: three hits, no runs. We scored twice off Vida Blue, one of the finest pitchers in the game and someone I had studied closely. We were a lot alike in how we worked. He wasn't especially tall or burly, but he was a lefty who threw fire and destroyed batters with a killer breaking ball. He was a big reason that Oakland won three straight World Series titles from 1972 to 1974. He was also from Louisiana, albeit a very different part of the state. Essentially, he was somebody I tried to model myself after, in more ways than one.

I took the mound in the ninth with that 2–0 lead and promptly gave it away. Home run. Out. Home run. Walk. As quick as that, it was 2–2, with the winning run on base. Out came Billy. The game was knotted up, and I was in danger of letting it completely fall apart. Sparky came in and got a double play to salvage the tie—and save my ass. Sparky didn't leave until the game was over . . . in the fifteenth inning. If I remember correctly, he joked that he crawled off the field, he was so tired, throwing six and two-thirds shutout innings before our bats put up three runs to give us a 5–2 win. I was upset because I'd given up the two bombs. But the bigger picture was that I had pitched well again. Good enough that there was no taking me out of the rotation. In my next four starts, I pitched well enough to get into the ninth three more times. I had pitched into the ninth inning in five out of my first six starts.

Which raised the question: When was Billy gonna let me finish one of these dang things?

———

That was the question racing through my mind during that start against the Royals. I had been pitching well. You don't consistently pitch into the ninth if you don't have good stuff. But each time, Billy shuffled out to yank me. Sparky asked me about it. So did Bonnie. I knew I was good enough to finish what I started. But Billy didn't seem to think so.

The game against the Royals, though, had a different feel. First, we had a commanding 7–0 lead. In a close game, I could understand pulling me: Sparky was the best damn relief pitcher in baseball. Give Sparky a lead, and you win the ball game, simple as that. And beyond Sparky being a mentor and teacher, I can't overstate the importance of knowing, as a starting pitcher, that I had Sparky behind me in that bullpen. Sometimes as a starter you can try to outdo yourself because you don't trust the relief pitchers to hold your lead. I never had to worry about that with Sparky. He could get ready at a moment's notice and shut the other team down. Most important, he could do that for several innings. You don't see relief pitchers like Sparky Lyle anymore. Today, most closers come in and get three outs. Sparky could come in during the middle of a game and finish it off. For him, that was routine.

Sometimes when I showed indications of tiring, giving up a hit or walk, pulling was the right thing to do, even if it was frustrating for me. This time, though, even after I walked George Brett to start the ninth, I knew I was still pitching well. All game, the Kansas City hitters couldn't touch me. This dangerous, powerful Royals lineup had just three hits against me. And with a lead so big, there was no reason to bring in Sparky. It would be a waste. Still, after I walked Brett, out came Billy. He was taking me out—or so I thought.

This time, however, the process didn't play out the same way. When Billy stepped out of the dugout, he usually signaled for the reliever immediately. At the same time, Thurman would time his walk to the mound to arrive right when Billy did. They'd tell me I'd done a good job and that was that. But this time Billy didn't signal. And Munson, instead of walking gingerly from behind the plate to reach me, burst into a jog to get there before Billy.

Thurman was our captain for a reason. You could describe him a lot of ways: tough, grizzled. More than anything, he was ornery. He didn't get along with everyone, but he didn't have to. His job was to lead, and what made him so damn good at it was that he always had the pulse of every situation, in the clubhouse or on the field. Understanding why he was so important had to do with smaller moments like this. He knew not finishing games was eating me up. He also knew Billy. And he was busting his ass to beat Billy to the hill to give me the lay of the land. He covered his mouth with his glove so nobody could see what he was saying.

"You have to tell him something. Tell him anything, or he won't let you complete the game."

"Okay," I told him. By not immediately bringing in a reliever, Billy seemed to be feeling me out. When he arrived moments later, he didn't say "Good job" like he usually did. Instead, he asked: "Well, what do you think?"

"You really wanna know what I think?" I said.

"Yeah, I really wanna know."

"I think you oughtta get your ass off my mound so I can finish my damn game."

Billy looked at me for a moment. Then he said, "Okay, you got it."

And he went back to the dugout. It was all a mind game, a test. It might sound brazen or stupid to challenge Billy Martin that way. But the truth is, that's exactly what he wanted to see. Billy was a brawler. He wanted his players to fight too, to burn with the same fire that consumed him. If you can fight me, he thought, you can fight anybody. And I wasn't afraid of Billy. I had been sent up and down to the minors, forgotten and abandoned in the bullpen, insulted and driven to the brink of quitting. Nothing could faze me. *If you're man enough to come out here, I'm man enough to tell you to get the hell out of my office.* And to tell the truth, I'm pretty sure that's what he wanted to hear. He wanted to know what I was made of inside. When I told him to get off my mound, I think it made him feel better. I got the next three guys out, for my first complete game, a 7–0 shutout. From that point on, he never took me out of a game again until he asked me how I felt. We established something between us in that moment that would allow me to anchor the New York Yankees rotation. Trust.

5

DID THE BRONX REALLY BURN?

Arriving at the ballpark every day in 1977, I was a witness to a type of theatrics the likes of which had never quite occurred in baseball history. While the drama—usually with George, Billy, and Reggie Jackson as the main cast, sometimes joined by Thurman—played out on the sports pages, on the radio, and on TV, drawing in the entire country, for us it played out live in the clubhouse, on the field, in the dugout. I'd get to my locker before the game, and it was like turning on the TV. When I'd leave, it was like turning the TV off.

You'd hear shouting and high voices. Billy and George going at it in Billy's office. The slamming of the furniture. Then Reggie walking in and the three of them going at it. Not every day, but often.

Everything that went on in the clubhouse that season has become so dramatized—literally, in the ESPN documentary *The Bronx Is Burning*, based on Jonathan Mahler's famous book about our team and New York City at the time. Now when we all get together, when I'm talking with Goose, Sparky, Willie, or Bucky, we ask one another: Did we really go through that shit? Despite all the sensationalizing, the answer is yes. And it was entertaining as hell. There was never a dull moment. It made me want to get to the park, just so I didn't miss anything. When I got there I'd ask, "What the hell happened last night after I left?"

Amid all of this, my personal journey—struggling to win a permanent spot in the rotation—was hardly front-page news. And that's how it was for most of us. We went about our business. Willie Randolph, Bucky, Graig Nettles, Chris Chambliss . . . you didn't see our names in the paper brawling with Billy or George. The rest of us just played the damn game. But that doesn't mean the drama was unimportant. It was.

The baseball season is long. There are 162 games across six months. Seven months when you add the playoffs. More than eight when you count spring training. If you don't have fun in this game, it'll drive you crazy. And we had a blast. And everything that went down, that's what made it so fun. In other circumstances, it might not have been fun. The reason it was, though, is that we went through all of it and still won.

I don't especially enjoy getting into everything that went on between the guys. For example, I respected the hell out of Reggie. And he respected me. At the end of the day, when we're together, we're the proud winners of two World Series titles for the New York Yankees. That's something special. And it wouldn't have happened without Reggie. So hashing through what went down that season, and the next, isn't to pile on about how ego and temper threatened to tear a great team apart. The point is to guide you through the underpinnings of our pinstripe legacy and show why it was so flammable. More than that, it is to understand why the fire never burned us down. There aren't a lot of teams that could've gone through what we went through and still end up winning the World Series. The 1977 New York Yankees did.

————

If you looked at me and Reggie Jackson in our uniforms, you could be confused that these two people played the same sport. I wasn't even six feet tall and weighed 150 pounds soaking wet. Nothing about me screamed that I was a freakish physical specimen. I looked like someone who could've spent the day riding a tractor or driving a truck. Because heck, I very well could've been had stuff played out differently. It's one of the mysteries of baseball that a string bean like me can throw ninety-five miles per hour, an overweight guy can hit forty home runs, or a little guy with quick moves can steal fifty bases. There's a place in the game for people you could pass on the street without batting an eye.

Reggie Jackson wasn't one of those people. He acted like a superstar and looked the part. He had those gold-framed sunglasses that looked like they came straight from a Hollywood movie set. His pearly, toothy grin was made for magazine covers. And then there was his physique. If you passed by Reggie Jackson on the street, you might not have guessed he played professional baseball. Football would've seemed more likely. While my uniform hung baggy and loose around me, Reggie's muscles fought through the fibers, protruding and showing the world just how strong he was. His arms were the size of my legs.

When George signed Reggie for more than $2 million, everyone knew what we were getting. First, there was the ballplayer, the one who hit thirty-plus homers per year, won the 1973 MVP, and mashed the A's to three straight World Series wins. Then there was the other side. The outsize personality who loved to see his face on television and magazine covers. The one who wasn't afraid to speak his mind in any situation. And when a player that talented, and that famous, says something—anything—it causes a media tidal wave. One of his more famous comments was that if he ever played in New York (this was when he played in Oakland), they'd name a candy bar after him. He'd be right up there with Babe Ruth and the Baby Ruth bar.

"I didn't come to New York to be a star," Reggie proclaimed the day he was introduced as a New York Yankee. "I brought the star with me." That was Reggie in a nutshell.

And that is what George signed up for when he rolled out the red carpet for his newest, most expensive acquisition in November of 1976. It was about a month after we had been swept by the Cincinnati Reds in the World Series, and George saw Reggie as the bat we were lacking, and needed, to take that next step and win a championship. There was no question his power would help. His hitting ability would help any team in baseball. But almost immediately there were concerns about how his personality would play in a clubhouse full of strong personalities.

In the clubhouse, Thurman Munson was our unquestioned leader. Not just in practice but in title: George had made him the first Yankees captain since Lou Gehrig was named captain in 1939. And Thurman rejected the very idea of a superstar on our team. We weren't some floundering mess of misfits in need of reclamation! We had just been in the World Series—yes, we had lost, but we were already a damn good team. That team, with some minor exceptions, was built on the backs of blue-collar guys in the trenches. We had good

players, and a few famous ones. But the biggest compliment
to that team was that out of twenty-five guys, there weren't
many superstars. We had twenty-five good players. That's
how Thurman looked at it.

Introducing somebody of Reggie's fame and outspoken-
ness, with a natural penchant for attention, was bound to
upset the delicate balance in the clubhouse. Meanwhile, the
balancing act between Billy and George was always shakier
than a wheelbarrow rolling over cobblestones. We antici-
pated the turbulence that followed.

The thing was, though, that the two Reggies—Reggie the
All-Star and Reggie the Superstar—were inseparable. It's why
he came to New York. The stories of how George wooed him
to New York are now famous: the walk along Fifth Avenue
where George sold him on not just the Yankees but playing in
front of Broadway and in the bright lights of the city. That's
why Reggie turned down more money to play elsewhere.
Only New York could satisfy both Reggies. George embraced
that, and that's why Reggie embraced George.

If Thurman was upset by this spectacle—and knowing
him and how much he valued hard work over fleeting fame,
I'd guess he was seething inside—he gritted his teeth at first
and played nice. He and Roy White put the Yankees uniform on Reggie at his introductory press conference. Thurman could be confrontational, but he wasn't going to create
a problem out of the gates. Besides, those months after the
World Series had already been a roller coaster for him. We
lost the Series; he was named the American League MVP;
he was publicly insulted by Sparky Anderson, the Cincinnati
Reds manager; and now the Reggie parade and charade.

Billy Martin wasn't Thurman Munson, but they shared

a great many values. They both believed in toughness. They both cared about playing the game right. The difference is that it's easy to see why, as the Yankees manager, Billy would have immediately taken Reggie's attitude as a personal affront. Billy was the leader of the team, not George. Billy was in charge, or so he thought. Bringing in somebody who had such clout with the owner, who wasn't known for busting his ass or being a hard-nosed player, was a direct challenge to Billy. Reggie was a great talent, but he didn't always play the game the way Billy expected his players to play it.

So that was the inevitable tension: Billy loved good ballplayers, but on some level he hated what Reggie represented. They were polar opposites. Reggie was hulking; Billy was scrawny. Reggie was made for TV or Hollywood; Billy was a loner. Reggie overwhelmed; Billy grinded. More than anything, Billy wanted fighters who would battle the other team and battle him. The only way Billy knew how to play as a ballplayer was by getting dirty and fighting for every inch, every hit, every base, every grounder. It wasn't pretty or flashy, but it's what worked for him. Reggie Jackson was about the glamor. That didn't fit Billy's vision, and he wasn't going to sit idly by and have that undermine his team. The fights between him and Reggie, him and George, were almost a foregone conclusion the second that contract was signed.

———

"I'm the straw that stirs the drink. . . . Munson thinks he can be the straw that stirs the drink, but he can only stir it bad."

—REGGIE JACKSON, *SPORT* MAGAZINE, JUNE 1977

Recounting each squabble that went on that season would serve no purpose. It was just too common an occurrence. And often it was the same stuff playing out over and over again. But there were a few key incidents that transcended the daily minutiae and became pivotal moments in terms of our survival as a team. That interview with *Sport* magazine was one of them, because it wasn't George and Billy bad-mouthing each other to a bunch of reporters. It was Reggie calling out our captain, our team, for the entire world to read about.

There had been constant battles about where Reggie should bat in the order. George wanted his star slugger hitting cleanup. Billy shuffled him around and usually had him hitting fifth or sixth. But as far as daily tension goes, that interview, printed for millions to see, brought it to a new level. It wasn't conjecture or tabloid speculation. Or George or Billy rehashing their same old fight about who was making the decisions. This was a feud between two players.

It's important to note that Reggie has gone out of his way in the years since to explain that he didn't mean it the way it came out in that article. That matters. But what mattered at the time was what it meant to us. And we interpreted it the same way everyone else who read it did. The message was clear: Now that Reggie was here, he was going to be the guy who leads the team. But we already had a good team and a good leader. We made the World Series. And Thurman wasn't just some guy with the title of captain, he was a world-class ballplayer. It was Thurman, not Reggie, who was the reigning American League MVP.

There's no telling how much this pissed off Thurman. He was used to being slighted, and he used that to fuel him. No

matter how well he played, there were always reporters saying Carlton Fisk, the Boston Red Sox catcher, was superior.
After the '76 World Series, Reds manager Sparky Anderson
was asked about Thurman and his catcher Johnny Bench,
who went on to the Hall of Fame. With Thurman next to him
at the news conference, Sparky said: "Don't never embarrass
nobody by comparing them to Johnny Bench." It was another
thing Thurman and Billy had in common. They both fed off
people doubting them.

The result of Reggie's comments about Thurman was
mostly the growing discomfort on the team. But at the end of
the day, their feud was strictly personal. It wasn't something
that affected our play on the field. And in any locker room of
twenty-five grown men, not all twenty-five are going to get
along. This was an extreme case of that. If Reggie was going
to spout shit like that, we would talk about it while we had
our coffee. There was no rule that we had to be friendly with
him. And Reggie brought that on himself. In fact, I'm not so
sure he was ever at ease after that incident. How could you be
when most of the other guys don't want to talk to you? But
even if he felt bad about it, there was no taking what he said
back. He knew that, and so did we. The only way to move on
was to win.

And Thurman, no matter how offended he was by something, was never going to let anything that would hurt the
team's chances at winning get in the way. Because that's what
Thurman cared about more than anything. If we won 161
games in a season, he would've asked why we didn't win 162.
So he didn't issue ultimatums or make the circus crazier. His
attitude, toward not just this incident but all the small things
too, boiled down to a simple philosophy: You and I are going

to play together, but that doesn't mean you and I have to like each other. Most of us adopted that from him. If it was good enough for Thurman, it was good enough for a guy like me, fighting for a job.

The team's reaction to Reggie was strictly personal, in that even if it made bus rides and hanging out in the locker room unpleasant for him, again, it didn't affect our on-field performance. Reggie still grabbed a bat and hit. Thurman still caught the games. They were doing what they could to win us ball games.

A few weeks later, though, things took a more serious turn. Because our problems actually started to threaten our chance at winning the pennant.

———

What happened on June 18—two days after my first complete game against Kansas City—is the moment people point to when they wonder, "How could a team dealing with that shit win the World Series?" The stakes were high. The drama out in the open for the entire world to see. And it centered on the two people you'd expect it to: Reggie and Billy.

Except this wasn't an instance of two people who just didn't get along having their feelings boil over. It wasn't clubhouse politics. Or some game of three-dimensional chess between Billy and George. In a very straightforward way, it was a matter of baseball.

Every game felt big for our team, but this stretch of the season felt especially important. We had gone from playing Kansas City, our toughest competition in the American League, to Boston. Any game at Fenway Park between the Yankees and Red Sox is intense. But these weren't just any games. The Red Sox were in first in the American League East, with us and the Orioles close behind. We had lost the previous day to them 9–4. So not only was it the biggest rivalry in sports, but these were the games that would go on to decide the playoffs. Sure, it was only June, but every single one mattered.

All you need to know is what happened in the bottom of the sixth inning. I was sitting on the bench, watching. We were down 7–4 with Mike Torrez on the mound, slogging through a rough start and just trying to get through the inning. He got an out, then gave up a single to Fred Lynn. Next Jim Rice stepped to the plate and hit a double to right field. At least that's how it would read in the box score. But this wasn't a booming Jim Rice double. It was only a double because of a disgrace that played out right in front of my eyes.

On the pitch from Torrez, Rice checked his swing. But his bat hit the ball anyway, and as luck would have it, it popped into shallow right field. Bad luck for us, but that stuff happens in baseball. The hardest-hit balls can be outs. Weak and accidental dinks can become hits. The problem wasn't the hit. It was Reggie's reaction to it. He dogged it. He leisurely moseyed over to it as if he were strolling across the front lawn to pick up the morning paper. He might as well have been wearing a robe and holding a cup of coffee. All the while, Rice's bloop stretched from a single to a double.

This had to do with baseball. It was an action with direct consequences that hurt the team. Bad outcomes are part of the game. I might throw a bad pitch, or Reggie might strike out. This was completely different. It was sheer laziness. Lack of effort. It straight up disrespected the twenty-four other guys who were busting their asses, scratching and clawing, to win every ball game. And if there's one thing Billy Martin would not tolerate, it was somebody letting his teammates down and letting the team down by not giving it his all.

As Billy went to the mound to take out Torrez, I saw Paul Blair, one of our backup outfielders, grab his mitt. That's when I realized something was out of the ordinary. It didn't take some sort of genius to put two and two together. Billy was replacing Reggie in right field. If any of this sounds obvious—on some level, sure, why wouldn't you bench somebody who did that?—it was far from routine. Pitchers leave games in the middle of innings all the time. Position players don't. Even if they are benched for one reason or another, it usually happens between innings. It's subtler. This was a public humiliation.

Here's the thing: If anybody else had dogged it like Reggie did, I'm sure Billy would've done the same thing. But because it was Reggie, the incident was magnified. He was the most talked-about superstar in baseball. The fights—between Reggie and Billy, Billy and George, Reggie and Thurman—had been playing out on the back pages of the newspapers all season. And in front of more than thirty thousand jeering Boston fans, and the millions more watching on national TV, Reggie had to walk back to the dugout, humiliated. The television cameras and every eyeball in the park and in the dugout were glued to him every step of the way. Because we all knew it wasn't over. Reggie and Billy didn't have much in common, but those two men spoke their minds. And they were about to have words. Or worse.

It didn't take long to escalate in the dugout. Both hurled f-bombs a bunch. Billy demanded to know what the hell Reggie was thinking. Reggie didn't see what was so egregious

about it, and wanted to know what the heck Billy was thinking. Reggie had been embarrassed. But at the same time, to
be truthful, I'd say Reggie embarrassed the entire team by
behaving like that in the first place. If they had been alone
in the dugout, I'm convinced they both would've left on
stretchers. Reggie was as strong as any man I've ever met.
Billy wasn't big, but his inner fire and fury made up for his
size and weight. Fortunately, we had guys in the dugout with
some sense to break it up before they could get that far.

But it got far enough for it to be a spectacle. What made
this squabble different from any of the others of the season
was how this played out publicly. This kind of crap played
out behind closed doors all the time on the club. They even
said crap about each other in the papers on a regular basis.
But this was an image, a film clip, that everybody could latch
onto. And that picture is how everybody saw the New York
Yankees. People thought we were a bunch of squabbling children instead of professional ballplayers.

Two things stood out to me about all of this, though. The
first was that even though we were a notorious circus, the
twenty-five players in that clubhouse handled it like men. By
the time the game was over and we were getting ready to leave
Fenway Park that night, it was over. Billy had done what he
had to, said what he had to say. Reggie had said what he had to
say. He had tried to defend himself and say he wasn't dogging
it, but everybody had seen it. Still, we might have looked like
children to everybody else, but we weren't going to act like
children with one another. We weren't going to come to the
park the next day and let that affect how we played. Tomorrow was a new day, a new game, a new opportunity to win.

The second thing is that this was a lesson our entire team

had to learn. Reggie had insulted the game of baseball. He had insulted his teammates. He had insulted the New York Yankees uniform. But my point, as crazy as it sounds, is that this wasn't about Reggie. It was about what it takes to win a World Series. And no matter how talented we were—and we had a load of good ballplayers—we would never reach that goal if every person didn't do every little thing during every single game. Good teams, even great teams, fall short all the time. So the infighting everybody else saw as dysfunction was actually hugely important. We had to confront our issues. It might've been easier to ignore them. It sure would've been less embarrassing. We would've had less explaining to do to reporters. But if we just let them fester, we would've never realized our potential.

———

Those kinds of lessons don't sink in overnight. That's why we didn't become a first-place team overnight. Boston finished us off the next day with a three-game sweep, part of a five-game losing skid. And sure enough, there were other times when our troubles crept onto the field. Less than a month after that game against Boston, some people thought Reggie acted too slowly on another ball in the outfield. But the biggest credit to this team is that there were so many people who didn't tolerate anything but the best. People didn't just sit back and expect Billy or Thurman to settle a problem. If Sparky needed to chew out Reggie, he did. Nobody was immune to criticism, and none of our leaders were afraid to dole it out.

And what ultimately made things click is that despite these high-profile lapses, Reggie truly did expect the best out of himself. That's why I ultimately respect him so much. You don't get to be an all-time great hitter like he was without a work ethic, drive, and unwavering will. He had that, and it showed in his numbers. No matter what was going on and how unhappy he was, he was hitting the baseball. He entered the All-Star break hitting .281 with sixteen home runs. Facts are facts, and he was helping us win ball games. As a team, we just needed to do the little things to go from good to great.

There were other factors taking shape as the season went on. That includes me. As much as I established myself and a level of trust with Billy during that complete game, this was still my first season as a starting pitcher. Bumps in the road were inevitable. At one point in late June and early July, we lost four out of my five starts—during the last of which I only lasted four and one-third innings while giving up six runs. But once Billy trusted someone, he trusted him steadfastly, and I wasn't about to let him down. The next time out after that start I threw my second complete game. This time he left me out there in a tight, 3–1 affair against the Brewers. He easily could have taken me out during the seventh when I gave up two walks and a hit, but I struck out the final batter of the inning, with the bases loaded, to get out of the jam. Then I retired the Milwaukee hitters 1-2-3 in each of the final two innings. Once I learned that Billy had confidence in me, I was never going to lose confidence in myself.

That also marked my first start after the All-Star break. It was a much-needed rest for me and my arm, with the results showing in that outing. It was also an important breath of fresh air after all the drama. But the beauty of everything that happened in those early months is that the air had been cleared and things were out in the open. Nobody was walking on eggshells waiting to trip the next land mine. You knew where you stood with everybody. You knew what was acceptable, what was expected, and what wasn't. And at the end of the day we all learned there was one thing we all cared about more than anything: winning.

When that happened, there was no stopping us. We started to play as a team, picking one another up, during August. All the other stuff became noise. It didn't matter to us that George's name was splashed all over the papers again, talking about how disappointed he was in us. "The thing that disappoints me most is the lack of pride the players have. They don't seem to care if they're known as the team that choked," he said.

Take my August 10 start against Oakland. We won 6–3 while I threw seven innings of one-run ball, but every little game, even against a low-quality team, showed our mettle and our growth. Instead of adding to the problems, Billy showed his faith in Reggie by hitting him cleanup that day against Vida Blue, a left-hander. Billy had rarely done that this season, and even sometimes sat Reggie against lefties. Reggie rewarded him with an RBI single in the first and another hit in the second.

Just like that, we started to win games every which way. During my next start, against the White Sox, I got hit hard and allowed seven runs in eight-plus innings. Then Sparky, who was our savior all season and would go on to win the Cy Young—an amazing accomplishment for a reliever—had a rare bad outing. Together, we blew a 9–4 lead and let Chicago go up 10–9. Then Chris Chambliss hit a two-run walk-off shot in the bottom of the ninth to give us the win. Reggie scuffed up his leg that day, but he toughed it out and played the next day. We were all picking one another up and turning into the behemoth we always thought we could be. We entered the All-Star break at 50-42, third place in the AL East and three games behind Boston. We went 22-7 in August and finished the month first place in the division, four games ahead of the Red Sox and the Orioles.

During these final two months I made another evolution. I went from being solidly in the rotation to becoming *the* guy the team could count on. On August 28 I celebrated my birthday with a two-hit shutout of the Rangers. It was the best, most dominant start of my career to that point. The next time out, I got another complete-game shutout, this time against the Twins. The following start, September 7 against Cleveland, I got hit around some early, but it just goes to show to what extent Billy believed in me. When I told him I was good, he didn't pull me, and I went *ten* innings. We won in extras. All of this built up to one last start of the season, against the Red Sox, who I hadn't faced all season. They didn't know what hit them in a 4–2 win for us, which marked a stretch of four straight complete games for me. I ended the season with a 16-7 record and a 2.82 ERA. As a team, we went 19-9 in September. That meant we won one hundred games on the nose. The playoffs awaited.

———

For the second straight year we met Kansas City to decide the American League pennant. The previous year we had beaten them dramatically on a Chris Chambliss home run. And these Royals, who I had faced in those pivotal moments earlier in the year, were still no fun to face as a pitcher. But after everything we had been through this season, we weren't about to become complacent in the playoffs. We had fought and fought all year, and through it all developed a toughness that would prove invaluable.

I started game two at Yankee Stadium. I should have felt a lot of pressure. We had lost game one at home, 7–2, and we couldn't afford to go down 2–0 with the series headed to Kansas City. But the funny thing was, I didn't feel pressure. That's not because I had ice in my veins or some cliché about remaining calm on the biggest stages. I have certainly felt pressure in my career. But everything I had been through this season had felt like a test, and I just kept passing. I proved myself in the bullpen. Then in the rotation. All I had to do now was show what I had been able to do for the entire season. It helped that we were at home, with the fans behind us in a stadium where I had grown comfortable.

Once I got through the first inning, I had that confidence. I walked Hal McRae, the second batter of the game, and he stole second with an error. That left George Brett and Al Cowens up with a runner in scoring position. Brett was a great hitter, but in particular on that day I didn't want to let Cowens beat me. He had finished second in the MVP voting, hit twenty-three home runs with 112 RBI, and I felt if I could retire him, I could retire the whole Kansas City order. Especially after he had three hits off us in game one. That loomed large in my mind. Brett flew out to center for out number two. Then I got Cowens swinging to end the inning. We won 6–2. I went the distance, allowing just three hits all evening.

After we split the next two, it all came down to game five of the five-game series. That's when Billy made a decision I couldn't really understand at the time. He sent me out there with just two days' rest. I could see why he wanted to use me. I was our hottest pitcher. But it's usually a tall task to go out there on *three* days' rest. Two is almost never done, and for good reason. I was stiff, still recovering from a complete game, and all of a sudden I was being thrust into action two days earlier than I was used to. I wasn't about to say no, though, even if I (and plenty of others) had doubts about the decision.

I knew it would be especially tough because there's a big difference between facing the Royals in New York and facing them in Kansas City. The turf at Royals Stadium made it a difficult venue for power pitchers. The ball moves faster than it does on grass, so they can just hit the ball on the ground and use that speed to their advantage. More ground balls become hits, and more singles become doubles. And that's pretty much what happened. I left in the third inning having given up three runs.

But it was also a day where we showed just how much of a *team* we were. I didn't get the job done, although I was given a difficult task. The guy who did, though, was Mike Torrez. Even though he had started game three, he had gone to Billy and said he'd be ready to pitch out of the bullpen if needed. He responded with five and a third shutout innings, an absolutely incredible performance.

What we did in the series with Kansas City often goes understated because of the offensive heroics that would follow in the World Series. But we didn't win this game, or the ALCS, without a string of key hits when it was all on the line in the ninth inning. With three outs left to save our season, we trailed 3–2. Paul Blair started it off with a single to center. Roy White, sent in to pinch-hit for Bucky Dent, drew a walk. Mickey Rivers followed that up with a single to tie it up 3–3. The next batter, Willie Randolph, then did exactly what we

needed by hitting a sac fly to put us up 4–3. We weren't striking out, and every batter was either getting on or advancing
runners. That sac fly won't go down as an all-time great hit,
but boy, should it. We added another run before the inning
was over. Not that Sparky needed it—he shut them down in
the bottom of the inning, and we were headed back to the
World Series.

———

My lone start during the '77 World Series came in game four.
In a seven-game series, the fourth game always feels like it
changes the course more than the others. It's exactly in the
middle, with three games before and the potential for three
after. We led the series 2–1, so a loss meant we'd be tied 2–2
with game five in Los Angeles, an opportunity for them
to take a commanding lead. A win meant we'd have three
straight chances to finish them off.

After that disappointing performance in Kansas City, I
had five days of rest and was on a mission to avenge my last
start. But it wasn't so much anger that motivated me, it was a
matter of proving something: that I could be better than I was
the last time out. Little steps. Each start growing off the last. I
had proven that all year. I just had to be myself, and with my
arm fully rested, that shouldn't be a problem. Not only that,
but game five in Kansas City had been an abbreviated one;
I had thrown only forty-five pitches. I was as fresh as I had
been all season.

The result was exactly what I'd hoped for. I went nine innings, gave up two runs again, same as in game two of the
ALCS, and I allowed only four hits. There were two key plays
that stood out to me. Both, looking back, gave a glimpse into

the future. Lou Piniella made a once-in-a-lifetime catch in left, robbing Ron Cey of a long ball and saving my ass. In the bright sun of Dodger Stadium, Lou casually got to the wall during the fourth inning, leapt, and came down with it like it was an easy schoolyard catch. It wouldn't be the last season-saving defensive play he made in a Yankees uniform. Two innings later, Reggie Jackson hit his first World Series homer as a Yankee to give us an insurance run and push our lead to 4–2, the eventual final score. And it wouldn't be the last homer Reggie would hit that October.

It's difficult to place the exact moment when we knew something special was going on. There was our being on the verge of winning our first World Series since 1962. Baseball, more than any sport, is a team game; we don't win it all without Lou's catch, Willie's sac fly, Sparky's Cy Young season, Torrez's relief performance, and a lot of little things that we could recount for days. But that day at Yankee Stadium, watching Reggie Jackson, you knew you were watching baseball history in the making.

Reggie was hot coming into the game, with home runs in game four and game five, even though we lost game five. It says so much about Reggie that he was able to put what he went through behind him to play the best baseball we had ever seen. Because even though a lot of the struggles were of his own doing, there's no discounting the fact that it was hard for him personally. But he put it all behind him to carry us to the finish. It started with a two-run shot in the bottom of the fourth, to take us from down 3–2 to up 4–3. Then he hit another in the next inning to make it 7–3. By the time he came up in the eighth, it's like we all expected it: us, the fans, folks watching on TV, anybody who was following the game. *Crack*. His third home run of the game. His fifth of the series. The nickname he earned following the game, Mr. October, may have started as a wisecrack but became the most deserved nickname in the game. Minutes later, we were celebrating on the field as World Series champions with a crazy story to tell about how we got there. Reggie and Billy hugged. Reggie and Thurman hugged. We all did.

6

LOUISIANA LIGHTNING

S parky," I said. "What's the earliest you've ever had to enter a game?"

It was June 17, 1978. We were in the Yankee Stadium bullpen, and I had just finished my warm-up pitches before a start against the Angels. The session hadn't been pretty. I had no idea where the ball was going. What separated me from other power pitchers wasn't just that I threw hard but that I did so with great control. For somebody who primarily relied on only two pitches—a fastball and a slider—perfectly spotting my pitches was crucial. And today I just felt like I didn't have it. Which for me didn't mean I was throwing the ball more slowly but that I had no idea where the ball was going. I'd aim low, but the fastballs would shoot up high and out of the zone. The sliders would bounce in front of the plate. No matter where I aimed, the ball wouldn't go there. So I wanted to let Sparky Lyle know he might have to come into the game early to bail me out.

In what had become routine before every game, as I'd leave the bullpen, Sparky would ask me how I was feeling. Sparky continued to look after me in '78 despite how tough the season had become for him. A mustachioed wiz out of the bullpen, Sparky was the best pitcher in baseball in '77. He appeared in seventy-two games, the most in the American League that season, had a 2.17 ERA in 137 innings, and won the Cy Young.

But before the '78 season, we signed another ace reliever, Goose Gossage. It's one of those things Mr. Steinbrenner didn't see right. It had nothing to do with Goose's personality or abilities. Goose is a great person and was an outstanding pitcher, as good as anybody in the game, including Sparky. Just twenty-six years old when he came to New York, he had already been in three All-Star Games for the White Sox and the Pirates. In '77 he had a 1.62 ERA. So when George signed him, he envisioned some sort of unstoppable two-headed monster at the back of the bullpen. Goose, the righty. Sparky, the lefty. Together, he thought, they'd be capable of shutting the door every night.

But the best closers, like Sparky and Goose, they don't match up lefty-righty. At the end of games, they expect to take the ball—they demand the ball. Being a great closer doesn't just take having filthy stuff. It takes having a certain bulldog mentality. And bringing Goose into the fold had the effect of neutering Sparky. Goose became the lead closer for Billy, and Sparky was cast aside. In his eyes he was underpaid and underused. He talked about quitting the game.

As a friend, I found it difficult to watch. Here was someone who had just been the Cy Young winner and a key reason we won the '77 World Series, and he was being treated like a broken-down has-been. That's what made his book about the 1978 season, *The Bronx Zoo*, such a breakout bestseller. It wasn't just about baseball or the Yankees. It gave a searing, honest picture of the mental and emotional turmoil he dealt with on and off the field that year. That cuts to the core of Sparky, because beyond being a once-in-a-generation pitcher, he was also a one-of-a-kind personality. He was famous for being a jokester—the times he sat bare-ass on someone's birthday cake or lit our shoes on fire. Yet beyond the slider throwing, tobacco chewing, and prank pulling, he was a world-class human being. And I was a grateful beneficiary of his wisdom and generosity.

Perhaps the biggest testament to Sparky's character is that no matter what, he always kept a close eye on me, asking me how I felt before each game. And on this day, the answer was not so good. "I've got nothing," I conceded. I had no idea why I felt that way. Maybe because it was so damn hot and humid that June day. The Bronx felt like a regular bayou. Or perhaps it had to do with the fact that even though my results had been good to start the season, I wasn't really in peak form yet physically and mechanically. Who knows? But regardless, one thing was clear: I had not the slightest clue that a historic night awaited.

On a New York Yankees team rife with craziness, I cherished stability in my own life. In some ways, that made me an outlier. During the '77 season I had become one of the better players. The core of the staff. But I kept as far away as possible from the drama that made our team so famous. Our other stars—Reggie Mr. October Jackson, Thurman Munson, Catfish Hunter, Sparky Lyle, Goose Gossage—had big-time, national reputations. But I just cared about pitching to the best of my ability and winning ball games. I craved something that you don't associate with those years on this team: security.

And for the first time, that's exactly what I had to start the 1978 spring training. I had signed a contract that, starting the next year, would pay me $200,000 per year. That didn't make me the highest-paid player around, by any means, but it was a huge sum of guaranteed money, back in 1978. When you toil away in the minor leagues, making pennies, inevitably you have doubts whether you'll ever make it. I had that. More than me, it was something Bonnie and the kids deserved after putting up with all my travels, minor-league demotions, and so forth—never knowing if it would pan out.

More than the financial aspect, though, knowing that I had a secure role on the team allowed me to prepare for the season. It put my mind at ease when, as usual, I struggled in spring training. When I was fighting for a roster spot in '77, that was a problem. A bad spring gave Billy a reason not to use me, or for the team to send me down to the minors. But in '78, for the first time, that didn't matter. Nobody doubted my role on the pitching staff. There were no more trade rumors, no more barbs from Billy or rants from George. I didn't have to worry about impressing anybody. When you're a rookie struggling during spring trainings, they doubt you. When you're established and you struggle during these exhibition games, the response is completely different. They say, he's a veteran—he knows what he needs to do to get ready. And as I've said before, for me spring training was process oriented, not results oriented.

I mainly threw fastballs at first, because my slider wasn't effective until my fastball was in peak form. I didn't care if batters hit 'em—the games were meaningless. So it wasn't a big deal to me when I had a late start to the spring because of the flu, and then got smacked for five runs in two innings during my first outing. My role was solid, and for the first time during spring training, my mind was at ease.

The other difference for me, this spring, was that for the first time I was preparing to be a starting pitcher. Although I wound up starting for most of the '77 season, I had begun the year out of the bullpen. That involves a different type of preparation, getting ready to pitch more frequently, although only for one, two, or three innings at a time. For a starter, the spring is important as a time to build up a different type of stamina. As the ace of the rotation, I was expected to go out there and throw nine innings. Certainly, that wouldn't happen every game, but it's the standard I expected of myself. That endurance isn't built overnight. It builds slowly, throughout the spring and into the early part of the season.

But because I got sick, my entire body calendar was pushed back. It made me arrive several days late to camp after I recuperated at home. Then, in those first exhibition outings, I still wasn't 100 percent healthwise. And so even though I had enough time to get my mechanics in order—I was throwing my fastball hard and my slider with bite—I hadn't ramped up to my typical endurance level by the time the season started. These things usually follow a progression: You might throw just a few innings in your first spring outing, then four the next time and five the time after that. By the time the regular season gets under way, your arm is strong enough to throw a full nine. Or at least close to it.

Instead, when Billy tapped me as the opening day starter, that timeline was delayed. I wasn't in full-throttle, regular-season form yet. I wouldn't be for a while. All of which made it difficult for me to predict, or expect, that the best season of my career awaited. As fate would have it, my 1978 season stands statistically as one of the best starting pitching seasons in baseball history.

————

The previous season, Billy and I had developed a strong sense of trust in each other. During any given game, when he'd ask me if I could keep pitching, the only reason he took my word for it was because I was always truthful. When I'd answer yes, that response only carried weight because he believed I'd say no when I thought I didn't have any gas left in the tank, or that I just didn't have my best stuff that day. If I wasn't straightforward with Billy about that, that trust would fall apart. Plus, I'd be hurting the team if I insisted that I stay out there even when I shouldn't. It's no good for anybody.

Because of where my arm and body were early in '78, I had to be frank with Billy often. Although throwing complete games, or close to it, had become fairly regular for me by the end of '77, I just wasn't physically there yet in April. Getting picked as the opening day starter despite not being full-strength was quite a statement of belief from Billy, and I had to reward that with not just pitching well but by not hurting the team by pretending to do something I couldn't. That was my mind-set in the early part of the season: gutting out solid, if unspectacular, performances that would give us a chance to win. To understand the 1978 season in its entirety, it's important to know that it began entirely unspectacularly.

That's how I pitched on opening day, April 8, in Texas against the Rangers. Starting the season down there wasn't ideal, considering my progress, because the last thing I needed when I was grasping for every bit of energy was having to battle the Texas heat. It's brutal, even in the early days of spring. And there were no domed stadiums in 1978. I fought my way through seven innings while allowing only one run, but it was tough sledding. All six hits I allowed came in the first three innings. When I left the game in a 1–1 tie, Billy had to make a decision that would come to define much of the rest of the season for us: Would he turn to Goose or to Sparky? He went with Goose, and that kicked off a rough start to the season for a player who would prove to be so instrumental to our success later in the year. Because as good as Goose was down the stretch, his first days in a Yankees uniform weren't pretty. He gave up a homer in the bottom of the ninth to Richie Zisk, a walk-off shot to send us to 0-1 on the season.

As it turned out, that would be the only time we'd lose with me on the mound for nearly three months. But during the early part of that stretch, it's not because I was dominant. Whatever my form, though, I fought my ass off to put us in a position to win every one of those games. Some days I might give up two runs, and at my peak, I could do way better than that. But our bats were more than good enough to score more than two runs and give us the win. But if I gave up four, or five, or six, then I'd be hurting the team. I refused to let that happen. I had to grind. We had to grind. We weren't as good as we could be during that first part of the season. But we all picked one another up—that's the hallmark of a great team. When I wasn't at my best, the offense could pick up the slack and seal the deal. Later I'd return the favor by throwing shutouts.

That's how it played out for the rest of April. In my next start against the White Sox, our home opener, I slogged through nine innings for a 4–2 win. But again it wasn't pretty. It may have been a complete game, but I allowed ten hits and struck out only four. That game was classic Reggie Jackson, or should I say, Reggie Jackson in a candy wrapper. Reggie hit a three-run bomb in the first. Because the last game we had played at Yankee Stadium was in the previous year's World Series, that made four homers in as many at-bats at Yankee Stadium for Reggie. And before the game, fans were given free Reggie bars. Yeah, he got the candy bar named after him after all. And when he hit that shot, all of the fans decided to throw 'em on the field in some sort of bizarre tribute or celebration that took the stadium staff forever to clean up. Thousands of orange wrappers covered the field. White Sox manager Bob Lemon called the whole display "horse manure." Nobody could have foreseen that Lem would be managing our team in a few months.

We won again my next time out, against Baltimore, and it was the same story. I was good enough but not overpowering. I gave up three runs in six and two-thirds innings. The final run was credited to me but came when Sparky allowed a bases-loaded walk to tie the game 3–3. Again, though, the bats picked me up. And again, credit to Reggie. He hit a walk-off shot off Tippy Martinez, our former teammate, in the ninth.

Then came what was probably the most uncomfortable moment of my career. In hindsight, it's a funny story. At the time there wasn't much funny about it. Beforehand, I looked at the calendar and saw that the game was scheduled for Monday night, against the Orioles. It was the game of the week, on ABC, and nationally televised. Howard Cosell was in the booth, the whole works. The nice thing about that meant my parents could watch the game from Louisiana. So I gave 'em a call to tell them they'd be able to catch it.

Look, parents are always parents. They still give you the same speeches they do when you're a kid. "Okay, Ronald Ames, this is national TV. Don't be picking your nose. Don't pick your ass, don't scratch your balls. Don't embarrass yourself and our family in front of the whole country!"

So that's what I was thinking about on the mound. And for most of the game, it wasn't a problem. The game was going along swimmingly. We raced out with eight early runs, and I kept the Baltimore bats scoreless, even though I wasn't striking many guys out. Up to this point in my career, I always pitched with a mouthful of chaw in my cheek. Levi Garrett was my chewing tobacco, and it produced big, juicy gobs of spit. Late in the game I let a runner on base and felt the need to spit. Usually that's no problem, but this time I started thinking about the camera on my face as I got the sign and looked down the runner. So I decided I'd wait until after the pitch, when the camera probably wouldn't be zoomed in on me, to let loose.

Well, I threw the damn ball, and it was a chopper right back at me. *Gulp.* As I reacted to the ball, the chaw, with all the juice, shot right into my throat and lodged there. Swallowing chewing tobacco is not a pleasant feeling. It's disgusting. I got the guy out, but afterward I stood behind the mound, hunched over. Everybody thought I was hurt. I was at an impasse: Do I try swallowing it, or throw it up for the whole world to see?

Fortunately, Catfish had once given me some sage advice on just this. I wasn't the first person this had happened to. "I'm gonna tell you this, and this is the truth," he explained. "If you ever get it down your throat, just go ahead and swallow it. Don't try to get it back up. If you try to get it back up, you're gonna gag. Swallow it and you're gonna get sick, but it's better than the alternative. Trust me, I know."

So I swallowed it. And nothing happened, right away. I didn't throw up, dry heave, nothing. Meanwhile, our trainer, Geno, is running out because he thought I pulled a muscle. "Gene, I'm not hurt . . . I just swallowed my tobacco." The whole scene concerned Billy, too, because it looked to him like I was hurt.

"What's the problem?" he asked. Geno explained the situation. "Oh shit."

I made my way back to the dugout after the inning. When I sat down, it all hit me. I was dizzy, my stomach felt queasy, and I let out an enormous "Ughhhhhhh."

Billy came up to me. "You think you can keep going?"

"As soon as I figure who to throw the ball to, yeah."

"Okay, you're outta here."

Thank you, Billy. We went on to win anyway. Afterward I was sick for three days. I couldn't eat, drink, or get anything into my stomach. Every time I'd smell something, I'd want to gag. But at least I didn't throw up on national television.

———

The results of my first four starts were pretty decent—I had a 1.82 ERA and we won three of them. But they didn't match the standards I'd set for myself. In three of the games, I had lasted only seven innings. I had just twelve strikeouts. Still, I knew I would get better. Slowly but surely, I showed signs of getting into my regular-season form.

We won my next two starts, against Minnesota and Texas, and both times I went six and a third innings. Not especially deep for me, but the encouraging sign was that I struck out seven batters in each of them. I had struck out more guys total in those two games than I had in my first four combined. I was fine with getting batters to make weak contact and letting our guys in the field make plays behind me. But when I was at my best, I was striking guys out, and that was starting to happen.

The other good thing that happened in those two games didn't have to do with me. Goose had had a dreadful start to the season. And when you're a high-priced off-season acquisition for the Yankees, getting the big bucks from George, it puts a lot of pressure on you from the media and the fans. For that first month, Goose was catching the brunt of that.

At one point during Goose's struggles early in the season, we had a minor run-in. It was a great example of how we interacted and were completely honest with each other. During a game, Goose had gotten up in the bullpen, and it looked like he might be coming in to relieve me in the ninth. At least he certainly thought so. But when Billy came out to the mound, I talked him out of it. I said that wasn't happening because Goose hadn't been looking good. I finished the game, but Goose was hot under the collar. Now, he and I were great friends—and we're even closer today—but that didn't stop either of us from speaking our minds.

Right after the game, Goose stormed into the clubhouse. He was steaming, still carrying all of his stuff from the bullpen. He took one look at me, and I knew exactly what he was going to say. I put my finger up before he could get a word in.

"Hold it," I told him. "I don't want to hear it. Until you start pitching better, you're not coming into any of my games."

He knew that, and I knew that. He just had a lot of

pressure on his shoulders after being such a high-profile ac-quisition. Goose, of course, went on to pitch *much* better for us. So after that, all either of us could do was smile.

That season, through his first six outings he had an 0-3 record and hadn't recorded a save. But in my last two starts, he came in for me in the seventh inning and took care of business. He got his first win of the season against the Twins, then a save against the Rangers. It was huge for him to get over that hump, because in New York, the longer a funk lasts, the more it gets magnified. He snatched that monkey off his back. It was also tremendously important for us as a team, because we needed Goose to be the dominating, intimidating force he had been in the past.

Over the following month, everything started falling into place for me. My May 13 start against the Royals came after I got a full week of rest between starts—a rare occurrence but a fortunate one that came due to a rainout and an off day. It allowed my body to recuperate from some nagging injuries I had been pushing myself through during the early days of the season. I went eight innings, fanning six, and allowed two runs in the win against a team that always loomed large on the schedule. The Royals were just as good as they had always been. That start kicked off a run of nine starts in a row where I went at least eight innings.

I knew I was in A+ form beginning with my May 23 start against Cleveland. It wasn't just that I threw a complete game, but I struck out eleven and gave up just five hits. My next start, against Toronto, was another complete game, and I didn't walk a single batter for the first time all season. Then I rattled off three straight starts with a combined thirty-one strikeouts and just two runs against Oakland, Seattle, then

Oakland again. That put me at 10-0 on the season in eleven starts. And we needed every single win. Our start was solid, but Boston's start was spectacular. Following that June 12 outing against Oakland, we were 33-24. Boston sat at 40-19, six games ahead in the AL East.

As satisfying as the run had been for me on a personal level, I knew it meant a lot to the guys who helped me get to this point too. Sparky made a running joke of it. He or Tidrow would turn to each other and say, "Oh no, we created a monster."

Or Sparky would say, "Gator's pitching, I can take the day off."

———

But I wanted to prepare Sparky on June 17 that this wouldn't be the case. And the start to the game against the Angels only confirmed my suspicions. Angels second baseman Bobby Grich roped a double to left field. The next batter gifted me a strikeout when he screwed up a bunt. Then Dave Chalk came within a foot of taking my head off with a screaming line drive right back up the middle. Fortunately, I was able to bat it down to get out number two. A strikeout ended the inning. No runs, but it took me a lot of pitches to get out of the inning because my ball was up in the zone. The second inning wasn't pretty either—I walked Don Baylor before getting a couple of fly balls and a strikeout to end the inning. Again, no damage done. Three strikeouts in two innings is a fine start, but that wasn't uncommon for me. And even though I struck out the side in the third, they were split by two singles. It hardly struck me as remarkable. Or the makings of a record-setting outing.

The tenor of the game began to change in the fourth inning. I could feel the command I lacked in the early innings settling into place. My fastball was zipping along the back of home plate. My slider bit hard and in the right spots against lefties and righties. But more than feeling it, I could *hear* it. I could *see* it. Because even before I realized my performance could be something special, the fans at Yankee Stadium knew it. I got two strikes on Baylor to begin the fourth, and some spectators got to their feet cheering in anticipation. *Clap. Clap. Clap. Clap* . . . swing and a miss, strike three. The next batter, Ron Jackson—same thing. Except even more fans were standing, creating an electricity around the field. Swing and a miss, strike three. Once I did the same thing to Merv Rettenmund to strike out the side, all of Yankee Stadium seemed to be on its feet. Nine strikeouts in four innings.

The single-game major-league strikeout record at the time was nineteen, set by three all-time greats: Steve Carlton, Nolan Ryan, and Tom Seaver. Ryan, by coincidence, was on the Angels and in the opposing dugout that day. No matter how well you're pitching, you never envision chasing the likes of those three guys. But what was even better than the thrill of chasing history was the energy and atmosphere and camaraderie in Yankee Stadium. I wasn't facing the California Angels alone. There were 33,162 hollering fans taking on history along with me. I can't overstate the importance of that. I had thrown a lot of pitches in those early innings, and in the prior few games, so I needed every ounce of energy I had. They gave that to me. Even more, their cheering intimidated the opposing batters. They had to contend with my fastball, my slider, and 33,162 pairs of clapping hands urging them on to their demise. Every time they got two strikes, I could see the surging anticipation in the crowd affecting the batter's body language.

And that's how my early success started to build on itself throughout the game. Each strikeout made the fans louder. And the hitters were more and more overwhelmed at the plate. They started swinging at fastballs up in the zone or sliders at their feet that they had no hope of connecting with. They'd stand like statues, watching pitches they should've been swinging at. I got Ike Hampton swinging for strikeout number ten in the fifth, then Bobby Grich looking for my eleventh. "Louisiana Lightning just struck," Phil Rizzuto, the former Yankee and our color commentator, said right around then. I believe a fan had come to the game with a LOUISIANA LIGHTNING sign, and he picked up on it. From there the nickname stuck.

The sixth inning was just like the fourth. Three down on strikeouts, all swinging. And they were against some quality hitters. Joe Rudi, their first baseman, had finished second in the MVP voting twice. Don Baylor, their left fielder and my future teammate, would go on to win the MVP in 1979. I had already struck out every batter in their lineup. My thirteenth strikeout was a new career high for me. The fourteenth put me one shy of Whitey Ford's Yankees record. I got that fifteenth strikeout to end the seventh, which sent the crowd into hysteria.

The thing was, even though I can count 'em looking back on it now, I had no idea exactly how many I had at that point. I knew I had a lot. And while I loved how much the fans were getting into it, I wasn't quite sure why they were going so crazy the entire game. There were probably only two people in the stadium who didn't know. The guys in the dugout mostly knew. The exceptions were me and Thurman. He and I were so focused on the game, attacking the batters and deciding the pitch selection, all we knew was that we had a 4–0 lead. When we were in the dugout, somebody told us to look at the scoreboard. It flashed that number: 15 strikeouts.

"Wait," Thurman said, pointing to me. "You? You have fifteen?"

I was just as surprised. But from that point on, I knew the stakes. I fanned Hampton again to start the eighth, setting the franchise record. That was my only one of the inning, though. Which meant to tie the MLB record, I had to strike out the side one last time in the ninth. That was the only inning where I went in with the mind-set of trying to strike batters out. Usually, that was just a product of me making good pitches. But for the ninth inning, even though I was tiring a bit after having thrown so many pitches, I couldn't help but try. For myself, but even more for all the fans. They were the ones who had given this June baseball game a playoff atmosphere. I had to give it my all for them.

And as quick as that, I got strikeout number seventeen to start the inning. The fans didn't sit down for the rest of the game. I didn't think the cheering could get louder, but sure as heck it did. Then I got number eighteen. Two outs, one batter left to tie the record. The tension ratcheted even higher when Baylor singled to center. But I ultimately fell one short. Ron Jackson grounded to third, ending the game. But I wasn't disappointed. I had broken the Yankees record, and the fans applauded me like they did in October.

"What an exhibition by the Louisiana Lightning man," Rizzuto declared on air.

The most gratifying thing about the game was its impact on baseball culture. Now if you go to a game, it's tradition, and routine, for fans to get on their feet when a pitcher has two strikes on a batter. That became a thing in baseball on that day. It's quite the feeling to be at spring training or watching a game and see that, knowing I had been a part of it. And that's not a credit to me but to the fans of the New York Yankees. I didn't start it. Yankees fans did. Their passion that day changed the atmosphere at baseball games forever. Which is to say, Yankees fans are the greatest fans in baseball for a reason.

My performance was also hugely important for the team. We were 37-25 after that win, fighting to stay within striking distance of Boston. And even though I had been bothered by the flu and a minor injury in those early months, I had yet to miss a start. I think all of our other starters, rattled by injuries, had missed a start or two by then. Those guys had been there to carry the team so many times, and pick me up, that it was important I do the same for them while they fought to get healthy again.

The start itself, in many ways, was a microcosm of my season up to this point. I started off slow and built my way into peak form. The game, to be sure, took a lot out of me. My arm was more tired after that start than it had ever been. But as it turned out, the best days for me and the Yankees this season were still ahead. The ironic thing is how my relatively light workload at the end of the previous season may have been the biggest blessing. I'm not a doctor or a trainer, but I believe I was stronger in September and October *because* I hadn't thrown as many innings in April. And to pull off a historic comeback against the Red Sox to win the AL East, we'd need to be as fresh as possible in those final days.

7

AND YOU THOUGHT 1977 WAS CRAZY?

By July 17, most of us had gotten used to how much of a circus the team had become. Heck, it was a year and a half old by then, and in that first year we proved we could persevere through it and win the World Series. And it was reasonable to think the situation would have improved over time. With more time, Reggie fit in more with the clubhouse. Even if we hadn't all become best friends with him, his most inflammatory comments were largely a thing of the past. He and Thurman had said their piece the year before. They'd high-five after one of them hit a homer; each was committed to bringing another World Series trophy to the Bronx. And beyond all of that, in sports, winning tends to solve a cartful of problems. And we had won it all.

But instead, our three-ring-circus act was only getting worse. Because despite our being the reigning World Series champions, and most of our struggles winning ball games having to do with injuries plaguing our team since the beginning of the season, we weren't winning enough for Billy and George. For a brief moment in the middle of July, we trailed Boston by fourteen and a half games in the American League East. As a result, the tension between manager and management was as bad as it had ever been. Oddly enough, though, it never once dawned on us that we couldn't catch the Red Sox. Yeah, we knew they were good. But we knew we were good too. Just as good as them. Still, we knew something had to change. The situation had to get worse for us to get better.

The wheels spun into motion during the tenth inning of a series finale against the Royals. Kansas City remained a measuring stick for us as one of the top teams in the AL, and we were coming up short. They took the first two games of the series by a combined score of 11–3. We had lost six of our last seven, and seven of our last nine, straddling the All-Star break.

Throughout all of this, Billy and George fought over who to play and where to bat 'em. There was a logjam in the outfield, and a lot of guys were unhappy one way or another. Either they were left out of the lineup, or there was unease because they were in the lineup at the expense of Reggie or somebody else. All the while, rumors swirled that Billy might get fired—as ridiculous as that might sound, considering he had just managed us to the world championship.

In this one game, all of our problems seemed to reach a boiling point. Sparky, unhappy all season about his role being usurped by Goose, expressed displeasure when Billy tried to use him as a long reliever. Goose, as a result, had to pitch the final three innings and gave up a couple of runs that tied the game in the ninth. That might've been enough problems for the day. But they got overshadowed by a dustup that infuriated Billy to his very core and brought our hellish situation to a point of no return.

Reggie stepped to the plate in the bottom of the tenth inning with nobody out and Thurman on first. Billy thought he could catch the Royals napping, so he called for a bunt. We didn't need a homer, we just needed one run to win the game, and nobody would expect a power hitter like Reggie to lay down a bunt. In fact, hitters like Reggie sometimes get insulted if they're asked to bunt. Regardless, he obliged. He fouled off the first attempt, after which Billy signaled to call the bunt off. But Reggie ignored the change. He squared up to bunt again—another foul ball for strike two. Billy seethed. To clear up any chance of a miscommunication, our third-base coach met with Reggie before the third pitch to reiterate that the bunt had been called off. Especially with two strikes, bunting made no sense because a foul bunt is strike three. Nonetheless Reggie bunted again, popping it into foul territory for strike three. We lost the game 9–7 in the eleventh.

Like the play against Boston last year when Billy pulled Reggie for dogging the ball in right field, this cut to the core of what offended Billy Martin's sensibilities. One of his players wasn't playing baseball the right way. The chain of command was being disrespected. Which was the whole problem in all the squabbles between Billy and George. Billy hated George's meddling in the day-to-day affairs, because Billy was the field manager. Now Billy's orders were being directly ignored by the one player who had already been the source of so much consternation.

After the game, Billy was understandably livid. He demanded that Reggie be suspended for the rest of the season. That was probably an overreaction, but he had reached the point where he just couldn't stand it anymore. It's him or me, he essentially told George. But not only did George have a particular affinity for Reggie, but like any owner, he felt he had to side with his high-paid slugger. Reggie was ultimately suspended for just five games. A week later Billy delivered his famous last line: "One's a born liar," he said, referring to Reggie, and "the other's convicted," turning to George.

The next day Billy resigned. But his "resignation" was a technicality. George was about to fire his ass. I had grown close with Billy, so it's difficult to admit, but it was necessary for the good of the team. I'd pitch the same no matter who was managing. But we needed to escape the craziness. We needed to put everything else aside and just play ball. And that's what we did. We needed for the next few months to right the ship. I'm not sure we would've been able to do that if Billy had stayed on.

———

At the start of the season, the personnel issues seemed small. Reggie wasn't Billy's favorite player, but he had become a better soldier. And there was no way to imagine things could get *worse* than the previous year. Billy pushing Sparky aside when Goose came on wasn't so much a teamwide issue—it had nothing to do with Goose as a person, or his abilities, or his effort. It just made me feel bad for Sparky, as a friend. The other was a short-lived rumbling that Thurman wanted to be traded to the Cleveland Indians, close to his home in Ohio. But nobody wanted to see Thurman go—not George, who had named him captain; not Billy, who respected his abilities and the way he played the game; not anybody in the clubhouse, who looked up to Thurman and valued his leadership. And Thurman was a class act who cared deeply about winning. He wasn't a problem.

Our struggles in the early months of the season had nothing to do with this. And it's not like we were playing terribly.

We had a mediocre April (10-9), a very good May (19-8), and a poor June (14-15). That adds up to a 43-32 record to start the season. But there were two factors that combined to make our record feel worse. First, since we had won it all the year before, the expectations for this season were sky-high. And second, Boston scorched its way through the early months. They were 52-23, or nine games up on us, by the end of June.

In '77 the Red Sox were already a good team. They won ninety-seven games, which is no surprise given a lineup that included Carlton Fisk, Butch Hobson, Fred Lynn, George Scott, Jim Rice, and Carl Yastrzemski. That lineup could stand toe-to-toe with any lineup in the majors. Their 5.3 runs per game that season trailed only the Minnesota Twins. The problem for them, though, was they lacked the pitching. We had a 3.61 ERA in '77, while theirs was a half run per game higher, at 4.11. That really was the difference in us winning one hundred games and taking the division.

So before the start of the 1978 season, Boston went out to address that. They signed one of our key starters, Mike Torrez, to a big deal to become one of the anchors of their rotation. Then, right before the season, they traded for Dennis Eckersley, a twenty-three-year-old All-Star from Cleveland. He was already making a name for himself and would go on to be not just an incredible starting pitcher but later one of the best closers in baseball history, which is how fans mostly remember him today.

Add Torrez and Eckersley to that already formidable lineup and they had quite a ball club. And all was going according to design for the Red Sox early on. They were hitting. They were pitching. They had depth. Their success was easily understandable.

We had the potential to be just as good, but there was a key difference. From the start of the season, we just weren't healthy. Even coming back from the flu and fighting through some minor arm troubles, I was the healthiest member of our pitching staff. Andy Messersmith, who we bought from the Braves and was meant to replace Torrez, separated his shoulder. Don Gullett had shoulder issues too. They made a combined thirteen starts all season.

The other issue was Catfish Hunter. He had hurt his back and shoulder, pretty much from the start of the season. But Catfish was a pro. I had learned a great deal from him—he was somebody I could relate to in a lot of ways. While he had become famous as one of the first of the high-priced free agents in Major League Baseball history—George signed him away from Oakland before the '75 season—he was at heart a good-natured country boy, who transformed himself into a menace on the mound. Like me, he liked to hunt. He didn't fancy himself at the center of a drama, nor did I. And he was a tremendous teammate.

Catfish was thirty-two years old by 1978, so on the field he didn't have the velocity or stuff he once did. There was a time nobody could match his pitching arsenal. He won twenty-five games for Oakland in 1974, earning him the Cy Young. In '75 he won twenty-three games for us with a 2.58 ERA. He won at least twenty games for five straight seasons. Even in his later years, with diminishing stuff, he could get guys out because he was so dang smart on the mound and knew how to work hitters. Pitchers like me could learn a lot just by watching him pitch.

But no amount of guts, heart, and smarts can overcome

fairly serious physical ailments. And that's what he was dealing with. He tried to pitch through it at first, but it was hard to
watch. His first start of the season he gave up six runs, including two homers, in just two innings. He went on and off the
disabled list that season, making just nine appearances in the
first four months, with an ERA of 6.51.

When you add in Goose's early-season struggles and
Sparky's banishment to middle relief, you're left with very little
stability on the mound. It was really just me and Ed Figueroa.
And while my performances started to command attention
because of my winning streak and strikeouts, Figueroa's success, too, deserves a lot of praise. He was just so consistent, it
was easy for some folks to miss. When I say the core of our
team was built not on the backs of superstars but on steady
performers who didn't need glamor, I'm thinking of guys like
him. He came to us in '76 from the Angels and won nineteen
games with a 3.02 ERA that year. He won another sixteen
games in '77 and had a Cy Young–caliber campaign for us in
'78 with twenty wins and a 2.99 ERA. He was a rock for the
team, taking the ball every fifth day and pitching well, throwing around 250 innings a year. He and I both made thirty-five
starts in '78. Nobody else made more than twenty-five.

The first time we went to Boston that season was in the
middle of June. Our starters were Ken Clay, Don Gullett, and
Jim Beattie. We lost the first and third games when Clay and
Beattie went a combined five innings and got shelled. Beattie would step up and come through in some big starts that
year, but he was a rookie. Nobody expected him to be starting those types of games when the season began. Clay mostly
came out of the bullpen. Meanwhile, the Red Sox started Luis

Tiant, Torrez, and Eckersley. At this point in the season, the tables were reversed from a year earlier. They had the health and the pitching depth. We didn't.

But our injuries weren't confined to the pitching staff. Willie Randolph, our second baseman, had a cartilage tear in his knee. He came to us in '76 after a cup of coffee in the bigs with Pittsburgh in '75; he and I were two of the young guys together. Willie was quiet, levelheaded, and unlike me found success immediately. He was an All-Star in both '76, his first full season in the majors, and '77. Although he didn't hit for power, he did all the little things exceptionally well. He played strong defense, could hit to all fields, and advanced runners. He also drew some of the most walks in the league in those years, which was so impressive because he wasn't a power hitter, so it's not like pitchers were deliberately pitching around him. He just had a great eye, taking walks when he could, long before on-base percentage was a statistic people looked at closely. And he turned those walks and singles into extra bases because he had a fair bit of speed, stealing more than thirty bases for us most of those years.

Thurman's knees had been deteriorating over the years. Not that he bitched and moaned about it. You had to fight Thurman to take him out of the lineup. He played 154 games, which would be a lot for any catcher—not to mention one who was constantly ailing. Sure more than any catcher plays these days. Naturally it was Thurman behind the plate during my eighteen-strikeout game—I wouldn't have had half as many with someone else calling the game, setting up the hitters. He made some of his starts as designated hitter to give his knees a break. And we started to play him in the outfield some.

All of these injuries added up to a very different team from the one we thought we had leaving spring training camp. And even though we were above .500, we were behind Boston by quite a bit. One of the biggest issues was in the outfield, where we started to have quite a logjam, as I mentioned earlier. We already had Lou Piniella, Mickey Rivers, Roy White, and Reggie. Plus Thurman was getting some games out there. Then on June 15 we traded for Gary Thomasson. Gary hit well for us, but with so many outfielders for only three spots, it created tension. When the lineup was posted, guys were uneasy, not knowing whether they were playing or not. Reggie, our best hitter and one of the best in all of baseball, all of a sudden found himself not playing every day. And he'd be pissed. Which made whoever was playing in his spot uncomfortable.

All of this—the injuries, the infighting, the unease around the clubhouse—kept building as we slipped further and further behind Boston. They kept winning, and we continued to play okay. And it felt like every couple of days, they'd gain another game on us. That's what triggered more radical moves with the lineup and added to the discord.

It was in this atmosphere that we hit the middle of July. We needed the All-Star break. The guys with bumps and bruises got a few days off to heal. That included me—the start against the Angels had taken a lot out of me, and I wasn't myself for a few outings. I probably shouldn't have pitched my last time out before the break in Milwaukee, but it's not like we had healthy arms ready to replace me. We lost that game 6–0, and I struck out only three, my fewest since April.

But within a few weeks everything started to change. We healed over the break. Within a couple of weeks, the fireworks finally exploded in the wake of the Reggie bunt incident. Billy was now gone. And finally, we could look at the standings and just think about baseball. We had a couple of months to pull off a comeback—and there was no doubt in our minds we could do it.

———

I never established quite the same relationship with Bob Lemon that I had with Billy. We didn't have as much time together and hadn't been through as much. He was our pitching coach in '76, but I was such a minor factor on that team, he didn't focus on me. Billy and I, for better or worse, had experienced a lot together and grown close.

As a player, Lemon had had a distinguished career pitching for the Cleveland Indians. He went to seven All-Star Games, won the 1948 World Series, and was one of the best pitchers of his generation. He led the major leagues in wins three times, struck out the most batters in baseball in 1950, and went to the Hall of Fame. He first managed in Kansas City, and then later for the White Sox. Before he left Chicago and before Billy "resigned," there were rumors that we'd just trade managers with the White Sox—Billy for Lemon. It didn't quite play out that way, but when Lemon got fired, George snapped him up quickly.

Lemon was an entirely different type of manager than Billy was. And as great a manager as Billy was, at this moment Lemon was a blessing in disguise. Billy was emotional and unsettling. Often that was good. This year it had become a problem. Lemon was a calming force. Everything about his demeanor was calm. He wasn't going to fight with the players or fight with George. He was levelheaded in everything.

That attitude changed the entire clubhouse. Before, guys had to tiptoe by the board to check out the lineup card to find out if they were playing or not.

With Lemon filling out the lineup, it was simple. You'd be in the lineup or you wouldn't—but it wasn't part of some long-standing feud or gamesmanship with George. If you were starting, you were starting. If you weren't, you were ready on the bench. "I ain't telling you how to play," Lemon would say. "I'm just gonna make the lineup. Read it. If your name's on it, give me your best." That's it.

For us, everything came together all at once. Finally, we were focused on just playing baseball. Even though we had a lot of ground to make up—fourteen and a half games with two and a half months left in the season—we had a team that was just as good as Boston's, if not better. We could catch them, and the situation in the clubhouse was finally stable. Even more important, we were getting healthier. The biggest difference in that regard might have been Catfish, who had hardly pitched in the first few months, and when he did, got hit hard. Starting with eight innings of no-run, three-hit ball on August 1, he was back to being the dominant pitcher who fooled hitters every which way. Over the final two months, he went 9-2 with a 2.23 ERA.

At the same time, everything that seemed to hamper us at the beginning of the year now started to hurt Boston. Over the course of the 162-game season, an entire team will never stay healthy the entire time. It just so happens that our injuries were stacked at the beginning of the season, while theirs clustered toward the end. Those injuries played a big part in their fall from grace. Rick Burleson, their shortstop, injured his ankle in the middle of July. They went 6-12 while he was out. Third baseman Butch Hobson missed a couple of weeks around then too, and played through an elbow injury for the rest of the year, which made him a major liability in the field. He finished the season with forty-three errors. Fred Lynn had an ailing back, Carlton Fisk's ribs got dinged up, and Jerry Remy had something wrong with his wrist. That's more than half of their lineup right there, going down the stretch. Some of them missed time, but even when they were on the field it was like what Cat was going through at the start of the year. They were just less effective.

Between us getting on the right track and their injuries, our results were reversed. The way they gained a game on us in the standings every few days at the start of the season, we started gaining those games back. By the end of August, we had made up more than half their lead. They finished the month at 84-48. We were 77-54. We still had to catch up six and a half games in September, but that was doable—and we had the chance to pull it off in one fell swoop because we played the Red Sox seven times.

———

Most of our strong play wasn't the result of anything extraordinary. We were just playing up to our potential, and doing so steadily. From the middle of July to the middle of August, I went nine innings in six of seven starts. Four were complete-game shutouts. Figueroa was going good, too; so was Cat. And Goose was well past the early-season hiccups and into prime form, which meant he was as good as anybody who has ever closed a baseball game. By early August, his ERA was below 2.00. We had a 3.55 ERA before the All-Star break. Afterward, it was 2.79.

Our charge set up what would turn out to be perhaps the most famous series in New York Yankees regular-season history. It became known as the Boston Massacre. Four games in four days at Fenway Park. Without our comeback in the division, though, those games wouldn't have meant much. Instead, they meant everything. At the start of the series, on September 7, we trailed by exactly four games. A four-game sweep—an idea that was ludicrous to even fantasize about, at Fenway Park—would leave us tied.

In games one and two of the series we didn't just beat them—we demolished them. We kicked the absolute crap out of them. Both games were over after just a few innings. The first game: 15–3; we had scored twelve runs before they collected their third hit. Torrez didn't even get an out in the second inning of that game before getting pulled. Second game, same story. We had eight runs before most of their lineup took an at-bat. They were thorough beatings in every facet of the game. We killed their pitching. They made mistakes in the field. Their bats were quiet, even though they were facing Clay and Beattie, who they hit around earlier in the season.

That left us with incredible momentum, a giant mental edge, and our two most consistent pitchers, me and Figueroa, going in the third and fourth games of the series. I was completely at ease on the mound, knowing how well our guys were hitting. Figueroa and I both won, with the offense scoring another seven runs in each game. The eighteen-strikeout game in June may have been my most famous game of the season. But that day in Boston I allowed only two hits—the fewest I had allowed all year. That is, until my next start, September 15, at home against the Red Sox, when I allowed only two hits again. By the middle of September, we had a three-and-a-half-game lead. Then they stormed back, winning their final eight. When we lost on the last day, we were both at 99-63.

Which set up the one-game playoff I told you about earlier. New York at Boston. Yankees versus Red Sox. Fenway Park. The most intense rivalry in baseball, and a playoff spot, all coming down to a winner-take-all finale on October 2. I was on the mound, on short rest. Yet given the fervor around the game, the wild fans, we weren't nervous. We had been through everything a team could go through that season. We'd just smacked the stuffing out of them *at Fenway* less than a month earlier. We had nothing to be afraid of. And the rest I told you. Lou's catch. Bucky's homer. Reggie's homer. We were going to the playoffs once again.

———

It's difficult to totally comprehend what you just went through in the moment. With time, you can sit back in your chair and reflect on how we came back and how crazy the season was. In the same way, I knew I'd had an excellent season, but it didn't hit me until afterward. I had a 1.74 ERA, a 25-3 record—there have been only a few pitching years like that in baseball history. Especially in the American League, after they instituted the designated hitter. It takes everything breaking perfectly. Same goes for understanding the historical context of that one-game playoff. We knew it was big, but only afterward did its place in time really resonate. We were happy, tired, and relieved all at once. But it's not like we had time to really process it. As soon as it was done, we were off to play Kansas City in the ACLS.

It was no coincidence that this was our third straight year playing the Royals in the playoffs. They had a strong team. But the confidence we had going into the Boston series we carried with us into the ALCS. We had proven that when we were healthy, we were the best team in the league. We resembled, in many ways, the Yankees team that had won it all the year before. It wasn't about any single person. On any given day, somebody would win us a game. We had a very deep, talented team. And Lemon was the calming element we needed to put it all together. With Billy, we might not have pulled off the comeback. Instead of explosive and contentious comments, we had a quiet swagger built on something simple: our abilities as baseball players to compete in every facet of the game. We could hit. We could pitch. We could play defense. We had mastered the fundamentals.

Beyond that, we felt like we had just beaten the only team as good as us in the American League. If Kansas City played in the AL East, they wouldn't have even finished in third. Milwaukee won ninety-three games to Kansas City's ninety-two. The fact that the Red Sox and the Yankees both had such good records in such a tough division—especially when you factor in the Orioles, another ninety-game winner—is a testament to how good we were in '78. If Boston had beat us in that tiebreaker, they very well could have been the team to win it all.

Because I had just pitched in the tiebreaker, I wasn't able to pitch early in the Kansas City series. Beattie, the rookie, got the call in game one. He combined with Clay to throw nine innings of one-run ball for a 7–1 win. They were prime examples of unsung heroes who played a critical role for us. Nobody was counting on them going into the year—they got pressed into duty because of injuries and ineffectiveness. But they both got better as the season wore on and had lower

ERAs in the second half versus the first. We lost game two 10–4 with Figueroa on the mound, but we were well positioned with the series tied 1–1, heading back to Yankee Stadium.

Game three was a battle between two of baseball's greats: George Brett and Reggie Jackson. Brett led off the game with a homer in the top of the first. Reggie tied it 1–1 with a homer to lead off the second. Brett homered again in the top of the third. Reggie tied it again with a single in the fourth. Then, you guessed it, Brett homered again in the fifth. Three at-bats, three home runs. We had so many big games against these Royals, and more to come in the future. But that performance was amazing.

The thing with our team, though, is we never let those things overwhelm us. Reggie, true to form, gave us the lead back with a sac fly in the sixth. We went down again in the eighth when Goose gave up a couple of runs, but again the Royals' lead didn't last long. Thurman stepped up with a two-run shot that ultimately gave us the 6–5 win and a 2–1 series lead. Battling through pain, Thurman had hit only six homers during the entire regular season. In big spots, though, he did what winners do, and what no cranky knees could stop him from doing.

That left game four to me, and I was feeling good after getting a full turn of rest. The one-game playoff against Boston was on short rest, as were some of my other September starts. With four days off, I owed my hitters a strong performance after they scored so much early in the series. And I preferred facing the Royals at Yankee Stadium. As I explained earlier, their team thrived in the fast conditions in Kansas City. I had more control of the game at home. They scored in the first after Brett tripled, followed by a single from Hal McRae, but that's all I yielded. I went the next eight innings allowing only four more hits. Graig Nettles and Roy White both hit solo homers—different day, a new hero. Meanwhile, Goose pitched a scoreless ninth to seal the win.

For the third straight year, we were going to the World Series. We wanted to make it two straight years with a trophy. A year before, we had been a circus, but we persevered. The circus was, if anything, wilder in 1978. It cost us our manager this time around. So we wanted to send another message: All of the craziness didn't matter. Once again, we were facing the Los Angeles Dodgers. We knew we were the best team in baseball. But proving it wouldn't be easy.

8

UNDERSTANDING YANKEES CULTURE

Dirty sons of bitches," Thurman huffed.

Contrary to what you might see in the movies, being a world-class leader doesn't necessarily involve standing up on a chair and giving a motivational, rah-rah speech. Thurman Munson wasn't just our captain in title. He was the best leader you could draw up for our baseball team. He didn't lead by giving us corny pep talks or lectures every day. He led by example. He led by playing damn near every game even when he was aching. He led by demanding excellence not just from himself but from the twenty-four other guys in the clubhouse. If I threw ninety-nine pitches for strikes, he wanted to know why the one hundredth was a ball. If we won six games in a row, he'd be irate that we didn't win seven.

Thurman didn't talk just to hear his voice, or because he thought it was the captain's job to do so. So when Thurman did speak, you stopped what you were doing and you listened hard.

And after game two of the Series, Thurman felt the need to speak up. He didn't stand up in front of his locker and demand everybody's attention. He just aired his feelings—his

anger at our play—to some of us in the clubhouse lounge.
There were seven or so guys there: Thurman, me, Graig
Nettles, Lou Piniella, Catfish, a couple of others. After everything we had been through in our 1978 season—the daily
altercations between George and Billy, Billy and Reggie,
and ultimately Billy's firing, Lemon becoming manager, our
comeback, the one-game playoff against Boston—we trailed
2–0 to the Dodgers in the World Series. He walked into the
lounge, poured himself a cup of coffee, and started talking.

"I wouldn't mind losing to those sons of bitches if we were
playing good," Thurman said. "Or if it was our first World Series. But goddammit, we've been here the last two years. We
won last year. We're the world champions. We're better than
the way we're playing.

"You see that little son of a bitch right there?" he said,
pointing at me. "If he wins the game tonight, we can go on to
win four games in a row. Then we got 'em."

We needed to be shook up. We were the defending world
champions. We hadn't played for shit for the first two games.
But that was in Los Angeles. Now we had three games in our
park. We should be able to win three games at Yankee Stadium. Then it's 3–2 and we can go beat the shit out of 'em
over there. But if we lost tonight, it would be a totally different
story. Our cages needed to be rattled. Thurman rattled them.

His message was simple. Forget the off-the-field stuff.
Not many teams come back from a fourteen-game hole in
the middle of the summer to make the playoffs. Especially
trailing a team as good as Boston. Yet, this is how we came
out of the gates in the World Series, playing a team we knew
we were better than? If we were playing an incredibly good
team like the Cincinnati Reds team that beat us in '76, that

would have been one thing. Thurman was saying he wouldn't mind losing the World Series to a team like that. But not to the Dodgers. We just weren't playing as well as we should have been.

Thurman talked about the team. He wasn't mad about how one person hit or one person pitched in the first couple of games. He wasn't telling Reggie that for us to win, he had to hit three more home runs a game. He wasn't telling me I had to throw a perfect game. He was saying we all had to chip in.

It reminded us about how it had been this season when we were at our best. You could look at our entire roster over the last two seasons and find games where every single person stepped up. That's what made us such a tremendous team. We helped one another, complemented one another, compensated for one another. It was an important reminder for us all that day.

Throughout the season, Nettles would come up to me on occasion when I was pitching and say he wasn't 100 percent. He never made a ruckus or begged out of the lineup. He played 159 games that year, after playing 158 the year before. He was our most consistent hitter, an All-Star who could hit for average and probably deserved an MVP at some point. Day in and day out, he produced for us.

But he would communicate to me when he was sore and might not have his usual range. Third base is a demanding position, because it requires a good arm and lightning-fast reaction times. By letting me know, I could adjust my pitching to try to cover for him. There are certain balls that are more likely to go down the third-base line, and I could do my best to avoid throwing those. He got so many important hits behind me, I'd do anything I could to help him out.

Before game three of the World Series, though, he didn't need any help. He told me he felt great. And his play saved my ass and our team. I didn't have the same overpowering stuff that I had most of the season. No reason in particular, but some days I just couldn't throw as good as others. But because Graig was feeling limber, and told me so, I could play to that advantage. When the guys behind you are able to make great plays, as a pitcher you don't care as much if you have great stuff, as long as you have good enough control. I kept throwing sliders in; they weren't as sharp as they had been most of that season, but Graig and the other fielders kept gobbling them up.

The box score in game three—nine innings, one run allowed—doesn't tell the full story of the game. I only struck out four guys. I gave up eight hits and seven—seven!—walks. I have never walked so many batters before or since in my entire major-league career. What made the difference was our defense. They just kept hitting the ball to Graig, and he kept picking them off. He started a double play in the second. He nabbed ground ball after ground ball, and I was happy to let the hitters keep hitting them.

We won that day 5–1. We won game four in the tenth on a walk-off single from Lou. Another game, another big moment when Lou stepped up. Beattie threw a complete game behind an offensive barrage to give us game five by a score of 12–2. As quick as that, we were up 3–2 in the series, with damn near everybody chipping in and doing their job, just like Thurman said. After we'd rattled off three straight, game six in Los Angeles felt like a foregone conclusion. We won, and for the second straight year, the season ended in champagne.

I would argue that the New York Yankees, as long as they have existed, have held a special place in American baseball lore that goes beyond our ability to win. The Yankees pinstripes are recognizable internationally. The navy blue, the NY, it's not just a uniform and logo, it's a brand, one that's as well known on the other side of the world as it is in the Bronx. The seasons, players, owners, and managers come and go, but the Yankees culture perseveres. That can make it difficult, and confusing, for people to pin the root of what sustains that culture.

One popular idea, especially in my era, is that it came from the top down. George was instrumental in reestablishing Yankees culture. He didn't just want us to play like champions. He wanted us to act like champions; he wanted us to look like champions. The rules he established after buying the team in 1973 are both famous and infamous: no long hair, no beards. To play for the New York Yankees, you're expected to look the part. We weren't part of a tree house, with a bunch of guys grabbing gloves and bats and messing around. We played for a world-class organization and had to act accordingly.

But to be truthful, I always saw it a bit differently. The Yankees culture wasn't invented in some owner's box and applied like sunscreen to the players. In fact, it was the other way around. The players themselves changed over the years, but their steadfast commitment to winning never did. It's an organization that has been blessed with uncanny leadership. Which is why I like telling that story about Thurman before game three of the '78 World Series. Our clubhouse culture wasn't what you read about on the back pages of the sports sections or heard about on the radio. It was about our day-to-day focus on accepting nothing but excellence.

Think of the players people recall when they think of the Yankees: Babe Ruth, Lou Gehrig, Joe DiMaggio, Mickey Mantle, Roger Maris, Phil Rizzuto, Billy Martin, Whitey Ford, Yogi Berra, Thurman Munson, Willie Randolph, Reggie Jackson, Mariano Rivera, Paul O'Neill, Joe Torre, Jorge Posada, Andy Pettitte, Derek Jeter . . . I could name fifty more in a heartbeat. In that group alone, though, you have ballplayers of every stripe. Some were charismatic and charming. Others would've been happiest if they never once saw their name in the papers.

But there are a few qualities that I have observed over the years that have defined the best Yankees leaders, icons, and stars—and as a result, our culture. The first is what Thurman showed us in the clubhouse: an unrelenting refusal to accept anything but winning. As a young player called up to the team in '75, I found having someone like Thurman as your catcher and captain completely changes your perspective. You demand the best from yourself because if it's not your best, or if you're not playing up to your standards, you're going to get an earful. That's a great thing for a team in any walk of life. To reach the top, to win back-to-back World Series titles, you need teammates who are willing to get angry when the team gets complacent.

That's something I saw a lot of on the great Yankees teams over history. Thurman Munson was tough—he'd get in our faces when he needed to be. But I'd describe Thurman as ornery. The Yankees of earlier eras, like the 1950s teams with Yogi, were *mean*. Beyond being a tremendous group of baseball players, that's what made those teams so good.

I got to know many of those players on Old Timers' Day, or when they'd visit the stadium. But I was especially lucky to see that on a day-to-day basis with Billy, and Yogi Berra, who was our bench coach (and later our manager). I had a close friendship with Yogi. But what I'll say here is what an incredible leader and competitor he was—even if he didn't have movie-star looks, or the easy eloquence you might expect from a New York star. Same with Billy. Neither was especially tall or good-looking. But they demanded nothing less than the best from their teammates, and later, as coaches and managers, from their players.

They wouldn't abide players not playing the game right. It is not a coincidence that the only baseball team ever to win five straight World Series had Yogi Berra on it. And Billy, too, for most of the run. I'm not sure there have ever been two smarter, more stubborn people to step onto a baseball field. Reporters and even teammates would make insulting jokes about Yogi's intelligence, and how he stumbled over his words. But Yogi was absolutely brilliant. As a hitter, he had a combination of power and contact that simply doesn't exist anymore. Some people ridiculed him for swinging at too many pitches out of the zone. But consider this: He never struck out more than 38 times in a season. He struck out just 414 times in his career and hit 358 home runs. This five-foot-seven catcher wouldn't let any pitcher beat him. Only one player in baseball history with at least 300 homers has fewer strikeouts, and that's Joe DiMaggio, Yogi's teammate.

As a catcher, Yogi made his pitchers' worlds better than they were without him, as Thurman did with me. And the numbers back me up. The ERA of the Yankees pitchers was better with Yogi behind the plate. He might be remembered for some funny quotations, but beneath that Yogi was a fierce competitor with an uncanny baseball mind, whose passion for the game fueled those Yankees teams. Here is just one example. When the Yankees were fighting for the pennant in August of 1951, Yogi had to be held back by his teammates, who were afraid he was going to sock the home-plate umpire after a ball-four call against the team. The entire team was stunned by his outburst. But it sent a clear message about just how much Yogi cared. Nothing got in his way.

To win day after day in the dog days of summer, year in and year out, you need somebody like that on the team to light a fire under your ass. A manager can only do so much, because he's not playing. It's best when that motivation comes from a teammate. When you flip through the generations of Yankees teams, the best teams had guys like Yogi and Billy and Thurman. The game has evolved over the years, and players who have that mean streak like Billy or Thurman are a rarer thing. They don't really make 'em like that anymore. But the Yankees championship team in the late nineties didn't just have the poetry and purpose in Derek Jeter. They had Paul O'Neill, who had that kind of fire. When I'd go to spring training as a coach, he really stood out. He would have fit right in with those older teams. I'd see him get red-faced and ride teammates, urging them on. Players like that, when they apply their passion the right way, are part of the glue that holds Yankees teams together.

Another defining aspect of Yankees culture, to me, is the unselfishness of the players who taught everything they knew to the younger players, the next generation. It's something I think about often, because I'm so grateful guys like Dick Tidrow and Sparky Lyle took me under their wing and helped to transform me into the person and pitcher I became. The thing is, they didn't have to do that. And they didn't do it begrudgingly. They actively sought me out. Which says a great deal about their character, because in some ways I was a threat to their jobs. While they were teaching me, I was a reliever. The better I became, the more dispensable they would be. But they didn't think like that. They saw a young player in need of guidance and stopped short of nothing to give me that.

The first time Sparky saw me throw, I was experimenting with a curveball and a slider. He was baffled. There's nothing good about having two mediocre breaking balls. It's much better to have one really good pitch. What he discovered was that I was getting bad advice from some of my coaches in the minors.

"Who's trying to help you down there?" he said.

"Well, nobody?" I replied.

When I was sent back to the minors, he and Dick would talk about how they just couldn't wait until I came back up so they could help me out. See, to Sparky it was paying it forward. As a young player with the Red Sox, he threw five innings and got dragged back out onto the field by Ted Williams, who wanted to talk to him about one of his pitches. He learned how to throw the slider to fool batters from one of the best hitters of all time. Then Sparky taught it to me.

They didn't just teach me the physical stuff, though. There were some strategic things that they passed on as well. Like how Dick would break down batters with me, and explain how to set them up, where to throw pitches, and when to throw which ones. On a day-to-day basis, veterans like Thurman, Tidrow, and Sparky showed you how to carry yourself as a professional baseball player. Which was never more important on a team that, at least in the public eye, didn't always act like professionals. In 1977–78 people sometimes thought we were a bunch of squabbling children. But contrary to perception, the way most of the players went about their business was as professional as it gets. They taught me to not get rattled. People could act like screwballs before games and after games. That's one thing. There were plenty of bad days in the Yankees clubhouse. They showed me you can fight one another all you want, but once that national anthem plays, you're fighting *with* one another. You're fighting to win, together.

Having veterans who lead like that creates a cohesive team culture. As players and competitors, we shared a belief in playing the game the right way.

It's one of the things that make Old Timers' Day at the stadium such a treat for me. Obviously, it was cool to see legends like Mickey Mantle and Roger Maris and shake their hands. But you also got to hear their stories and learn from them. They didn't just ride off into the sunset when they were done playing. It's something George understood, the importance of having the former stars and players around, whether for Old Timers' Day or down in Florida for spring training. Think about the resources I had around me as a player. Not just Thurman, Sparky, and Billy Martin. Yogi Berra, our bench coach, had the locker next to me. Next to Yogi was all-time great Elston Howard.

These guys weren't just great baseball players, they were world-class teachers of the game. As a player, I routinely walked into the clubhouse, sat down at my locker, and faced Yogi. "I'm pitching today," I'd say. "Tell me something." He always had something. As great as he was as a player—ten-time

World Series champion, three-time MVP, Hall of Famer—
you had to *drag* stuff about him out. He was humble that way.
But ask him for pointers or advice on the game of baseball?
He was a walking encyclopedia. He'd always have something
to offer about one of my pitches, or approaching batters, or
the mental aspects of the game.

9

THE LOSS OF A LEADER

Thursday, August 2, 1979, we had the day off. I was at our New Jersey home with Bonnie and her folks when the telephone rang. It was Mr. Steinbrenner; there was no mistaking his voice. He seemed to gather himself. "This is George. In case you have not heard, Thurman was killed in a plane crash." Simple. Straightforward. Heartbroken. I later learned he was flying his Cessna Citation with flight instructor David Hall and a friend, and had crashed short of the runway. Thurman was all of thirty-two.

"Just try to make your way to the ballpark around three thirty. We're going to have a meeting, make arrangements. We'll talk about it when you get there."

He only called a handful of us. Me, Cat, Graig Nettles, Lou Piniella, a couple of others. I called Goose and Bucky. At first there was nothing to say. We hadn't just lost a great baseball player. We hadn't just lost our captain. We hadn't just lost the man who led us in two back-to-back World Series wins. We had lost a friend. A family had lost their father. You think about what it would be like if it happened to your own family. You know all your teammates are thinking the same thing. It affected everybody in ways that went far beyond baseball.

It made you feel the game isn't as important anymore. That's human nature. It made the entire 1979 season a blur, gray, hazy. It's all clouded by that one memory. We finished with a fine record, 89-71, but fell short of the playoffs. I went 18-8 with a 2.78 ERA. But who really cared about the numbers when Thurman had died so tragically?

Thurman was buried the following Monday in Ohio, with most of the Yankees in attendance. After the funeral we flew back to play the Orioles on national television. I was on the mound that day; our catcher was Brad Gulden, a young guy without much experience. He stayed in the dugout until after the national anthem was played, out of respect. All four umpires stood on either side of home plate. Normally, during the anthem, Thurman would be at home plate, and I'd be looking at the flag with my hat off. As the anthem finished, it hit me. I looked to home plate and saw it was empty. Thurman would never be there again.

It's probably the only game I ever started in which I just didn't care whether we won. I went through the motions. But I just didn't feel connected to the game. I pitched a complete game, but it wasn't anything special. I gave up four runs and struck out nine.

But it was a special day for Bobby Murcer. Bobby had first come up with the Yankees in 1965 as a nineteen-year-old. Like Mickey Mantle, Murcer was from Oklahoma, and a lot of people hoped he would be the next Mantle. He'd had some great years with the team in the early seventies, before I got there, then bounced around from San Francisco to the Cubs in '75. We traded back for him in June of '79. Going as far back as he did, he was one of the players who knew Thurman best. Earlier that day he had delivered the eulogy at Thurman's funeral.

When we were down 4–0 in the bottom of the seventh, Murcer came up and hit a three-run homer off Dennis Martínez. *Okay, shit,* I thought, *we're back in this.* Our emotions were all over the place. Then Murcer came up again in the bottom of the ninth. Bucky had walked to start the inning. Willie got on, and they both advanced off an error. Second and third, nobody out. Bobby knocked a walk-off single to left field, scoring both of them. It seemed fitting. Thurman had been at the center of so many of our comebacks. It wasn't a happy moment, to be sure, but it was fun to win it. That's what he would've wanted.

I call 1979 our "I Don't Care Year." I couldn't tell you where we were in the standings on any given day. I try not to think about that season because it brings up so many memories. Looking back on it, it makes me think about how much one *person* can mean to a team. What he can mean to the twenty-four other guys in the clubhouse.

The clubhouse without Thurman was not a fun place for a long time. It just didn't have the same vibe it had when he was alive. His locker was at the end when you walked into the locker room; from where I was, he was catty-corner. To get to the training room, either you went through the bathroom area or you passed right in front of his locker. Every time you'd pass, he'd always have something to say. As gruff as he could be, he was funny as hell. He'd pick on the young kids. He was serious but good-natured.

And he'd let you get away with a lot, within reason. But he was pretty much a stickler in one thing: What goes down in the clubhouse is one thing, but on the field it's another. If things in the locker room weren't going good, he voiced his opinion. And we needed that. At the same time, go look back at pictures or video from '78. If Reggie hit a homer, Thurman was the first to congratulate him. If Thurman hit a homer, Reggie would be the first to congratulate him. If you asked them if they disliked each other, they had the perfect response: "Yeah, but not on the field."

Thurman's skills and knowledge of the game were exceptional. But what really separated him was that he understood everybody's psychology. As a catcher, he had the unique ability of knowing what it took for each pitcher to get through the inning or the game. There were some guys he had to coddle. Some guys got better if you poked them or pissed them off. He knew exactly what he had to do to get each of us to perform. I was one of the guys he tried to piss off. I got better when he made me angry. I was all right without being pissed off. But if he got me worked up, I got better. I'd throw the ball so damn hard I actually tried to hurt him. He knew exactly what buttons to push.

One day I gave up a home run and he trotted up to the mound. "Goddamn," he said. "He hit the dogshit out of the ball. Anything that flies that far oughtta have an airplane ticket attached to it."

Another time he walked out to me, pointed to the sky, and said, "You ever notice how clouds make all these strange formations and shit?"

"What the hell are you talking about?"

"That one over there looks like the pitch you just threw that went out of the frickin' ballpark like a cannon shot."

Sometimes, to send a message, he'd tell me to throw a fastball right down the middle of the plate. I thought he was crazy. But who was I to disregard him? I'd do it, and sure enough, the batter would miss. Thurman had a point: He was showing me I was good enough that even if I threw it down the middle, they couldn't touch me. It built me up. He might tell a batter what pitch I was throwing and where. If they didn't hit it, it sent the same message. At the same time, because he was mostly telling the batters the truth, they believed what he told them. So when there was a pitch we really needed, he'd lie to the batter. Then the batter really had no chance.

It made my job as a pitcher so much easier knowing I didn't have to do much thinking on the mound. He knew all the hitters, he knew me. I could just throw the ball. He was always going to call the right pitches—I didn't have to shake him off. To get me to shake him off, he had to give me a different sign, instructing me to move my head sideways just to keep the hitter on edge, to keep him guessing at what I was going to do. One time when I accidentally shook him off, he called time and came out to the frickin' mound.

"What the hell are you doing?" he barked at me.

"I was just trying to clear my head," I replied.

"How the hell am I supposed to know?"

The whole pitching staff benefited from his knowledge of the game. When Goose got off to a rocky start in '78, Thurman knew just how to handle him. The first time they had met was when Goose was on the White Sox. I read that after

he hit Thurman with a pitch, Goose got a note from him following the game saying he didn't feel a thing. Goose, after all,
was a hell of a pitcher, and it's not like he lacked for ability. So
Thurman kept it light, maybe got him a little angry and motivated, and it worked out. He'd hand Goose the ball and say
something like "How you gonna screw this game up?"

———

Our team would never go on to win another World Series
while I was with them, and you have to think it begins with
losing Thurman. I don't mean just the sadness and heartache
we had to cope with in '79. We were having a fine year, but
we likely weren't going to make the playoffs regardless, because we were too many games back. However, in the bigger
picture, we lost everything when he left. The leadership that
defines generations of the best Yankees teams, willing them
to reach their potential, that was gone. There were other great
players there, but not the clubhouse leader we had in Thurman. Lou Piniella was a terrific and dedicated player. Nettles
was, in my mind, one of the best of all time during his years
with us at third. But they weren't Thurman. I was coming
into my own as a veteran, but I sure as heck wasn't Thurman.
Nobody had his combination of skill, smarts, personality,
toughness, passion, and leadership. We had lost something
we simply couldn't replace.

Often catchers make the best managers. From their van-
tage point, they see the entire game. All the fielders are out in
front of them. They have to work with the pitcher, and they
bat. Thurman would've been a damn good manager. And
one aspect that made it more difficult going forward into the
eighties was that some of the other great baseball minds who

could've helped guide us through it weren't given much of a shot to do so. When we weren't winning the way George wanted, he didn't give those guys a long-enough chance. Those were people like our manager Dick Howser, who George summarily fired after the 1980 season, or Mike Ferraro, who he basically got rid of in the middle of a playoff game. Everybody got fired in the eighties.

The way people got to learn from Billy and Yogi after they retired, I just knew they would've done the same with Thurman. But that's why while I pause here to talk about his passing, it's so important to share the qualities that he had that propelled us to two world championships. So many of the Yankees who shared a clubhouse with him know the impact he had.

10

THE ALMOST YEARS

In many ways the 1979 season began a new act in my career. I had experienced so much, and so quickly: toiling away in the minors, almost quitting, and then overnight success. Despite the squabbling and managerial changes, the one constant was that we won. In '76 we reached the World Series. In '77 and '78 we won it all. But it wouldn't always come so easy.

Even before Thurman's death, 1979 had a different feel to it. During the spring of 1978, we were all fired up after winning that first World Series. You walk in the first day and everybody is high-fiving, talking big about doing it again. There was an electricity in the clubhouse, as we looked forward to April and getting our World Series rings. We had signed Goose in the off-season, and the thought of having two dominant relievers pumped us up. And in general, spring training was usually fun. During the first couple of weeks, you're done before noon and can enjoy the Florida weather. We'd go bass fishing in Lake Okeechobee or play golf. Starting in 1977, Bonnie and I would rent a house. Jamie, our eldest daughter, was born in November of '76, and we needed a bigger place. Some years we rented one right on the beach.

But '79 began with a strange tenor, because we had traded Sparky to Texas during the off-season. He had meant so much to me, and had done so much for the team, it was odd arriving there and not seeing him. In some ways I was happy for him, because he would again be the closer. I could never for the life of me figure out why he'd been treated the way he was treated the previous year. A season after winning the Cy Young, it was like he was invisible. He deserved a fresh start with a team that could appreciate him.

There was a lot of pressure on me after my performance in '78. That was a magical season, and no matter how well I pitched, expecting to duplicate that would be unrealistic. Winning that many games with that good of a win-loss record and that low of an ERA requires everything falling perfectly into place: me pitching my best, my teammates making incredible plays behind me, the offense giving me big-time run support throughout the season, and so forth. So a lot of my personal statistics that season are really a credit to my teammates. The Cy Young Award was just as much ours as it was mine individually.

Regardless, the season raised my profile nationally and raised expectations along with it. What would I do for a follow-up performance? Could I do it again? People seemed to expect that. Either I'd go out there and do it again, or my arm would fall off from throwing so hard and so much.

Since I had been a starter for the Yankees, I had been blessed with an incredible bullpen behind me. It's so important for the staff, having guys like Goose and Sparky who can throw not just one but multiple innings of shutout ball. Not to mention other stalwarts like Dick Tidrow. It gave me a great security blanket, knowing that even if I didn't go all nine innings, I could trust the guys who I was handing the ball to. It's one of the many things that made us so good as a team.

But in 1979 our bullpen went into flames, and quickly. First we traded Sparky. Then Goose hurt his thumb during a brawl in the clubhouse with Cliff Johnson, who played some designated hitter for us and backed up Thurman behind the plate. It started off as a joke when Cliff was asked if he could hit Goose when they played against each other. Goose replied with something like "only when he could hear it." Goose was saying that he threw so fast, Cliff couldn't see the ball. Now, these were two big men; both were six foot three or more. Goose threw a ball of tape at Cliff, and halfhearted, joking, and playful shoves devolved into an actual fight. Goose was out until the middle of July. We traded Cliff to Cleveland.

Last, in May we traded Tidrow, my other mentor out of the bullpen, to the Cubs. Goose's injury had pressed him into being one of our late-inning guys, and that wasn't the ideal spot for Tidrow. He had mainly been a starter in '78, with guys like Cat hurt for stretches, and when he was in the bullpen he was best suited as a long-relief man. In shorter outings he struggled. I felt Bob Lemon didn't put him in positions to succeed, leaving him high and dry out there. One day Tidrow told Lemon his arm was bothering him and he couldn't keep going. In Tidrow's final two outings for us, he threw four and one-third innings, allowing fourteen hits and nine runs.

Bottom line, Sparky was gone, Tidrow was gone, and Goose was injured.

As a result, I offered to pitch out of the bullpen. Some in the media questioned that: Why in the world would you put the guy who had one of the best seasons in baseball as a starting pitcher in the bullpen? Some speculated it could be bad for my arm. But my offer was approved by Al Rosen, our general manager, George, and Lem. We needed somebody to get outs, even just here and there. And I was happy to volunteer. I wasn't concerned with records or trying to appease people's expectations. I wanted to do what was best for the team, and that was that. It's how we operated in the clubhouse. And I know my teammates appreciated that. "You're showing me a lot," Reggie said to me after I volunteered. That, in turn, meant a lot to me.

I always maintained that I could be an even better reliever than I was a starter. I threw only two pitches, and I could be even more overpowering if a batter only got to face me once in a game, as opposed to two, three, or four times, when seeing me throughout the game might help him figure me out. In shorter stints, I could throw harder, too, without having to worry about going a full nine innings. Before I became a starter, I had proven myself as a star reliever in Triple-A. I knew I could do it well.

It also helped settle me down mentally. Whether it was the pressure on me or just a short funk, I can't really say, but I had a 5.25 ERA after the first two starts of the season. That's only a couple of games, sure, but I had only four strikeouts total. It's possible I was letting things get to me. After that I made a relief appearance and got a clean save. Then I moved back to the rotation with two complete games, allowing just one run in each. It cleared my head, loosened my arm, whatever, it helped. I made a couple more relief appearances in May, and I threw six and one-third innings without allowing a run.

We finished the season 89-71, which was respectable, but fourth place in our division, and thirteen and a half games behind Baltimore. Billy was brought back as manager in the middle of the season. It wouldn't be the last time he'd go in and out of the job, but for now I enjoyed having him back. But again, to me the entire season was colored by Thurman's death.

———

During the off-season, I invited Jim Spencer, a first baseman who played for us and was a big power bat off the bench from 1978 to 1981, down to Louisiana to show him a good time and give him a taste of our way of hunting. He came for a few days, but I'm not sure he knew exactly what he was getting into.

I picked him up at the airport, and he had supper with me and my family before we hit the sack for a couple of hours before heading out to our hunting camp for a few days. Jim had hunted plenty before, but he had never been hunting in Louisiana, and he was a little nervous.

"Mr. Guidry," he asked my father before we left, "you think we'll see alligators? Water moccasins?"

"Oh yeah," my dad said. "You're going to see them, Jimmy. The best advice I can give you is to just stay close to Ronnie."

I didn't know about that conversation, and I didn't quite realize yet just how nervous Jim was. During our ride to the camp, where we picked up my cousin Joe, Jim kept asking, "You think we're gonna see a couple ducks?" I was wondering why the hell he was asking if we'd see a couple of ducks. The thing was, I had never stopped to consider how different it was where he hunted up in Maryland. There, they'd go out by a lake and on a good day would see two ducks and on an excellent day would hit one. Louisiana was a different world. There were hunting limits on how many we could shoot based on the type—mallards, pintails, wood ducks, gray ducks, wi-geons, blackjack ducks, and so forth—but we could see hun-dreds or even a thousand or more in one shoot.

"Oh, you're in for a real awakening," I told him. "Jim, you're going to miss a lot more than you're going to shoot at, I can promise you that."

The great part about hunting isn't the hunting itself, though. It was the bonding, spending time with someone, getting to know them.

It was still dark when we arrived at the camp. I got out to get some stuff from the back of my truck. You could hardly see a thing, but I turned around and Jim is right behind me, sticking to me like wallpaper. He made me nervous with how close he was, following my every move. "What the heck is going on?" I asked him.

"Your dad told me wherever we go, stick close to you."

At this point, I could finally see how nervous he was. It was just different from what he was used to. We got in our mud boat and started toward the blind we'd be hunting from that day, which was about twenty minutes away. We had Jim sit in the front of the boat so he could take in the scenery. At one point, there was a sharp turn and you could get thwacked by all the tall reeds if you weren't careful. So Joe grabbed Jim on the back to yell above the boat's motor. "Jimmy! Watch your face!"

Jim feels Joe's hand on his back and shoots right up. Then he gets smothered by all those reeds. When we got to the duck blind, he looked like a damn Sasquatch with all this stuff sticking to his body. He was as white as a napkin.

So to get into the blind, you had to crawl through a little hole. When we told Jimmy that, he refused.

"You came here to hunt—why the heck not?" I asked.

"I think I crapped my pants when you grabbed me back there! I was thinking some creature could reach out from the grass and drag me into the bayou and nobody would've ever heard from me again."

After laughing our asses off for the next ten minutes, we eventually got into the blind and began the actual hunting. At one point, Joe nudges me. About twenty yards away, he points to a bull alligator meandering through the pond. The thing looked like a damn submarine. But all he was doing was patrolling his territory—you could tell because he was maintaining the same speed as he swam by. He wasn't any threat to us. But if I thought Jim was nervous before, he was almost jittery now. I guess he reacted pretty much the way anyone would who had never seen a huge bull alligator up close before out in the swamp.

"If that thing comes another foot closer, I'm out of here."

Well, we had a great hunt and got back in the boat to come back. As we slowed up around the curve, I saw one of the biggest water moccasins I had ever seen. Must have been eight feet long. And where Jimmy sat in the boat, he couldn't have been more than a few feet away. Like a lot of creatures when they are startled, water moccasins like to puff themselves up and put on an intimidating front. So this water moccasin opens its mouth wide, showing off its white mouth—its other name is cottonmouth—and those big fangs. But it had just been swimming in the bayou, minding its own business. It wasn't actually a threat to us.

We spent a few more days hunting after that, but poor Jim saw everything he wanted to see in those first few hours. He got the full Louisiana experience. We'd talk about it all the time during the season. And for my part, I loved giving people a taste of where I was from.

––––––––

By 1980, I was the only guy on the starting pitching staff left from 1977–79. Catfish was done after a tough '79. We traded away Jim Beattie. Figueroa struggled and got traded to Texas midway through the season. Goose, who I had grown close with, was the most familiar face left. Willie Randolph, Bucky Dent, Graig Nettles, Lou Piniella, and Reggie were still there. Chris Chambliss got traded to Toronto. Mickey Rivers was sent packing too.

And after missing the playoffs in '79, Billy was let go again. Dick Howser became our manager in 1980. He had been one of our coaches for a long while, so we were familiar with him, and it didn't require a big adjustment on my part. He didn't have a big personality like Billy, so we didn't have to master a new kind of circus. So many of the managerial changes were just George being George, and George and Billy doing their thing. My attitude was, just give me the ball and I'll pitch. It didn't affect the way I played.

Through all of it, we had the makings of a very solid baseball team. We signed Tommy John, who at age thirty-seven had an incredible season for us, winning twenty-two games with a 3.43 ERA. His name has since become famous because he's the namesake of the elbow ligament surgery that every pitcher seems to need these days. To us, he was a key veteran presence solidifying a pitching staff that going into the season didn't have much certainty beyond me. He was on those Dodgers teams we faced in the World Series, and we were glad to have him now. The other savior for our pitching staff

George and I had a pretty close relationship over the years.
(Rusty Kennedy/ Associated Press)

In the clubhouse with Dave Righetti (left) and Sparky Lyle.
(New York Daily News)

With all-time Yankees great Mickey Mantle.
(Courtesy of the author)

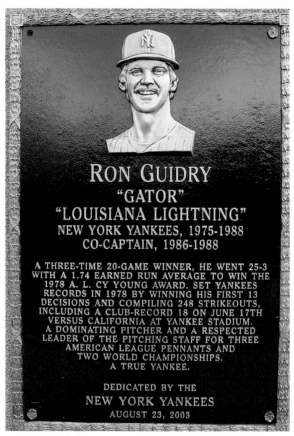

RON GUIDRY
"GATOR"
"LOUISIANA LIGHTNING"
NEW YORK YANKEES, 1975-1988
CO-CAPTAIN, 1986-1988

A THREE-TIME 20-GAME WINNER, HE WENT 25-3
WITH A 1.74 EARNED RUN AVERAGE TO WIN THE
1978 A. L. CY YOUNG AWARD. SET YANKEES
RECORDS IN 1978 BY WINNING HIS FIRST 13
DECISIONS AND COMPILING 248 STRIKEOUTS,
INCLUDING A CLUB-RECORD 18 ON JUNE 17TH
VERSUS CALIFORNIA AT YANKEE STADIUM.
A DOMINATING PITCHER AND A RESPECTED
LEADER OF THE PITCHING STAFF FOR THREE
AMERICAN LEAGUE PENNANTS AND
TWO WORLD CHAMPIONSHIPS.
A TRUE YANKEE.

DEDICATED BY THE
NEW YORK YANKEES
AUGUST 23, 2003

On August 23, 2003, I was honored when the
Yankees retired my number 49 and dedicated this
plaque in Monument Park in Yankee Stadium.
(New York Yankees)

With Goose Gossage at spring training, helping to teach a new generation of players. *(Courtesy of the author)*

Watching a game with bench coach and former teammate Don Mattingly (left) and manager Joe Torre, during my stint in 2006–2007 as the pitching coach for the Yankees. *(Getty Images)*

Congratulating
Mariano Rivera
after a save when
I was the Yankees
pitching coach.
(Getty Images)

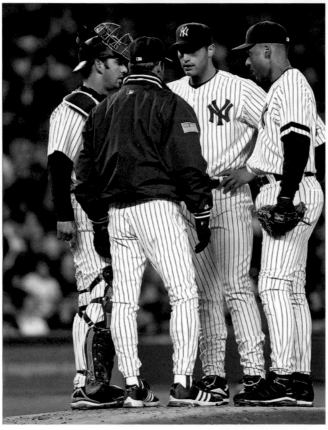

A quick conference on the mound with Andy Pettitte, along
with Derek Jeter and catcher Jorge Posada. *(New York Yankees)*

With Alex Rodriguez during spring training. *(Mike Carlson/Associated Press)*

With Andy Pettitte before the start of a game. *(New York Yankees)*

In the dugout in spring training, after all-time great Yogi Berra gave Nick Swisher some hitting advice. *(New York Yankees)*

The last game played in the old Yankee Stadium, on September 21, 2008. From left: David Cone; Goose Gossage; Helen Hunter, widow of Catfish Hunter; "Chairman of the Board" Whitey Ford; Don Larsen; me; and David Wells. *(New York Yankees)*

With my buddy Yogi. *(Courtesy of the Yogi Berra Museum)*

With Dave Eiland, manager Joe Girardi, and Willie Randolph before the final game at the old Yankee Stadium. *(New York Yankees)*

With Tino Martinez at the Yogi Berra Museum Celebrity Golf Classic.
(Courtesy of the Yogi Berra Museum)

The Guidry family (from left): my daughter Jamie; son-in-law Mike; my wife, Bonnie; my son, Brandon; my daughter Danielle; and son-in-law Jerrid.
(Courtesy of the Yogi Berra Museum)

Frying frog legs for spring training.
(Courtesy of Lily Hawryluk)

was Tom Underwood, who we got in the trade with Toronto for Chambliss.

The other part of that deal, however, was more important. We acquired catcher Rick Cerone. Rick had his best season at the plate in 1980, hitting fourteen home runs with 85 RBI. Even more critical was his presence behind the plate. Nobody could replace Thurman Munson at catcher, but Cerone brought a lot of good qualities. In the final two months of '79 without Thurman, that's when you realize just how much he did for the team, and how much pressure that took off me as a pitcher. I didn't have to think on the mound with him back there. He knew the opposing hitters better than I did. Heck, he knew my pitches better than I did. He could tell me which pitch to throw and where to throw it, which made it easy.

Cerone brought some of the same attributes. Coming from Toronto, he was familiar with the batters we'd be facing. For a twenty-six-year-old, he had a lot of experience already and knew how to set up as a catcher, how to call a game, how to manage the pitching staff. It was also comforting that Cerone was a tough, old-school type of player. That's what you want in a catcher, and it helped our entire pitching staff that we had somebody we could trust back there.

When you put all of that together, we had a good ball club. And things felt relatively stable. When we fell to 3-6 to start the season, we didn't panic. By the middle of May we had taken the lead in the division, and we wouldn't give it up for the rest of the season. Talent-wise, it may have been the best team we had while I was there. It was a damn good, all-around team.

While people get caught up in Reggie's antics in '77 and '78, mostly because of Billy and the off-the-field stuff, it is easy to forget how good a player he was. And amid everything, he had become a good teammate too. As a hitter, his performance in 1980 was one of the best I ever saw. At an age when you might expect him to decline—he was thirty-four—he only seemed to be getting better. Graig Nettles, on the other hand, was thirty-five and played just eighty-nine games, while batting .244. Father Time catches up with all of us in this game, and it's never fun to see it happen to somebody you've played with for so long. It happens to different people in different ways. Lou Piniella was thirty-six in 1980 and played 116 games, but he'd lost a lot of his power, with only two home runs.

Reggie, though, had his most complete season as a Yankee that year. He played 143 games, hitting 41 home runs with 111 RBI. He hit for average, batting .300 for the only time in New York, and walked 83 times. He was patient, powerful, and productive. Maybe the spotlight having dimmed a bit helped him, now that Billy was gone. But he was always a tremendous hitter. In some ways, it's ironic. A couple of years ago, Reggie had been the center of so much drama. Now he was our steadiest player. He deserves a great deal of credit for that.

My 1980 season was in many ways reminiscent of 1979. I was good but not dominant. I went 17-10 with a 3.56 ERA, respectable numbers, though it wasn't as smooth as that. During the middle of the season I hit a tough patch and straightened myself out in the bullpen. As a reliever, I pitched in eight games with a 1.96 ERA in eighteen and one-third innings. Some pitchers view going to the bullpen as an insult or a demotion. To me, it was a new opportunity to work things out and help the team. I'd have played outfield if that's what they thought was best.

It all added up to a 103-59 record, the most games we'd ever win while I played for the Yankees—the most we won since 1963. And once again we were set to face the Royals in the playoffs. But in 1980, George Brett was better than ever. Which is saying something, because he was damn good every other year, too. To emphasize how good he was that year: He played just 117 games and still won the MVP over Reggie, hitting 24 home runs with 118 RBI, and a .390 batting average. Incredible.

As many times as we had beat Kansas City in the playoffs, it was just their turn that year. After returning from the bullpen, I was tapped as the game one starter against the Royals. For the first time, we lost a playoff game that I started. For whatever reason, I had no control that day. It might've been the worst game I ever had. I had issues locating the ball, walking four guys in three innings. Only thirty-nine of my seventy-five pitches went for strikes. It was very uncharacteristic. When I wanted the ball inside, it ended up away. When I wanted it low in the zone, it was above the batter's head. I gave up four runs, and we were eventually swept, 3-0. It stank. But I felt the Royals were due against us. The sun can't shine on the same dog's ass every day.

In some ways I wondered if the 1980 season felt too easy for us. We won 103 games. Baltimore challenged us a bit for the division, but we were really able to coast the second half—we were that good. At our best, though, there was no coasting. In '77 and '78 we were always on our toes, for better or worse. Billy made sure of that. Thurman made sure of that.

And the finicky nature of baseball is that you can be the best team in baseball for six months, but if the other team is better than you for a few days in October, that's that. And that's what happened. For three days, they were better than us. As tended to happen when we didn't win it all, Dick, our manager, was fired. That's just the way it was.

If 1980 with the Royals was a case of what goes around comes around, that's what happened to us again against the Dodgers in 1981. Losing to them in the World Series was a bitter pill to swallow, more crushing than losing in the playoffs the previous season. At the same time, 1981 wasn't like a true baseball year because of the players' strike in the middle of the season. The strike meant the playoffs had this weird format, with the winners from the first half of the season playing the winners of the second half.

George's shiny new toy during the off-season was Dave Winfield, the All-Star outfielder from San Diego who signed for $25 million, a record at the time. He acquitted himself well in the shortened season, with 13 home runs in 105 games. But in general our bats struggled. I'm not sure if it's because we had a hard time getting into a rhythm or if age had caught up with some guys, but our bats were quiet. Willie, who'd had perhaps his best year in 1980, struggled in '81. Rick Cerone wasn't the same hitter again either. Graig Nettles and Reggie were a year older and didn't have their best season.

What we had, though, was our best pitching ever. That's how it was with so many of our teams. Different days, different heroes. In 1980, Reggie, Willie, and some of the other guys picked us up. This year the pitchers were in peak form. I pitched in 23 games, starting 21, with a 2.76 ERA. I had some of the best command I ever had, with only 26 walks in 127 innings. Tommy John had another marvelous season at age thirty-eight with a 2.63 ERA. And out of nowhere, a twenty-two-year-old Dave Righetti, who as a minor leaguer was part of the trade for Sparky, had a 2.05 ERA in 15 starts. All three of us were lefties, and we gave other teams fits.

When we gave our bullpen a lead late in the game, the other team could forget about it. I didn't pitch one complete game, but we had George Frazier, Dave LaRoche, Doug Bird, and Ron Davis in the bullpen, and all had sub-3.00 ERAs. And Goose, boy, I had never seen him be so lights-out. In 46.2 innings, he had a 0.77 ERA. He gave up only four earned runs all year.

The strange playoff format meant we had to go through two rounds to reach the World Series. The first was a series between us and Milwaukee, the two teams that won the AL East during the two halves of the season. They took us to five games after we won the first two. I pitched game one and game five, and neither went particularly well. I didn't get through the fifth inning either time. But I didn't get hit really hard, either, and with our bullpen there was a lot less pressure on me. Goose saved all three of those wins, as we won the series 3–2.

In the ALCS we faced Oakland. But the matchup wasn't billed as much around the Yankees versus the A's. Everybody seemed to pay attention to the man managing in the opposing dugout: Billy Martin. He did a great job with that Oakland team, but our pitching was too good for them. They scored four runs all series, in a three-game sweep. I didn't pitch because I had pitched game five of the series before.

The World Series brought us face-to-face with the Dodgers,

again, the team we had beaten to win it all in '77 and '78. Whenever I see Tommy Lasorda, their manager, he says to me, "Aw, we should've beat your ass three times." I always tell him they won the one they deserved. It was especially fitting for them, because it was the exact reverse of '78, when they had a 2–0 lead and then we won the final four games. This time we took the first two and then they cleaned us out.

I pitched well in game one, seven innings and one run. What still eats me up is I pitched so damn well in game five but still lost it. That day in Dodger Stadium I had everything working. I had my velocity, my command, my slider, all working. Lou gave us a 1–0 lead with an RBI single in the third, and it was one of those days when I felt it might be all I needed. Through six innings I had allowed only two hits. To start the seventh, I struck out Dusty Baker on three straight pitches. Then I got ahead of Pedro Guerrero, and *thwack*. Solo shot to left center. Next batter, I had Steve Yeager on a 1-2 count, and *thwack*. Solo shot to left center. I struck out nine, walked only two, and felt like in most respects it was the best game I had ever pitched in the playoffs. But it was the worst time to make the worst pitch, twice in a row. We lost the series in game six.

It was frustrating. And of course, we didn't know it was the last time our team would ever win a pennant during my career. But, look, how do you think those other guys felt when we won and they lost? Sometimes you need to take the good with the bad, the bad with the good. The game can bring you way, way up. And it can humble your ass.

11

LOSING BUT LEADING

The Sunday before the All-Star break in 1985, I was at my locker taking a nap. That was often the case for me on days when I started. I liked to get a little bit of rest before loosening up, to make sure I was fresh. We were a few games back of Toronto in the AL East standings. It was the last game before the break, and George felt the need to stress the importance of this game. And George had one way of doing that. He marched into the clubhouse, found me snoozing, and slapped me awake.

"*Hey,*" he bellowed, his finger in my face. "I don't want to tell you how big this game is. We've got to have this game. We can't lose it. You've gotta have a great game. You've gotta win this for us."

I had to get up in about ten minutes anyway, but he'd just taken ten minutes out of my nap. And hell, he'd just slapped me. I was not happy. I was hardly awake and still orienting myself. When I finally had my senses, I responded in the only way George would have wanted me to respond.

"What the f—k are you doing in my locker?" The entire clubhouse was watching us. "Get your ass out of my locker. Get out of our clubhouse. Get back in the f—king office where you belong. I don't come into your office. Don't come into mine."

We screamed back and forth a while longer. It was mostly "you mother" from him and "you mother" from me. What I noticed, more than anything, was his outfit. He was wearing a yellow turtleneck with a pair of beige pants and a green jacket. Not like the color jacket you get for winning the Masters. It was an uglier, lighter green.

So I turned around before he left and added: "When you leave here and get back in your office, take that ugly frickin' jacket off. You look like a damn parrot."

He was red in the face as he stormed out. The entire clubhouse started laughing.

A week or so later, when we were back from the All-Star break, it was still all anybody wanted to talk about. I was back at my locker goofing off, drinking some coffee. Somebody asked me if it was true that I'd called the old man a big frickin' parrot. I said yes. Standing not too far from us was George's driver, Bobby. After everybody cleared out, Bobby came up to me.

"Well," he said, "after that happened, the old man came upstairs into his office. I was sitting on the couch, and he threw the jacket at me. George goes, 'Goddammit, Bobby, put that frickin' jacket in the closet. Don't ever let me wear that jacket again. Gator said I look like a big frickin' green parrot. Make sure I never wear that back into the locker room.'"

But here's the thing about George Steinbrenner: That's exactly what he wanted to have happen. He'd rather you tell him to screw off than to not say something. Not unlike Billy. Say anything, but say something. Just don't say nothing. Sure, he ranted and raved like he was the king of the world. He always thought of himself as the toughest son of a bitch who walked this earth. He figured if you'd fight him, fighting the other team would be a piece of cake.

He was a master motivator. If you got embarrassed when he chewed you out, that was your problem. But everybody seemed to respond on the field. If he said you're not hitting home runs, the guys usually started hitting home runs. If he told me I sucked and wasn't pitching well, I started winning. You wanted, more than anything, to prove that he was full of shit. And he got exactly what he wanted.

It was all in good fun, too. One second we'd be cursing at each other. The next minute, if we bumped into each other in the hallway, outside the view of the rest of the team, he'd put his arm around me. "How's Bonnie? How's Jamie? How's Brandon? How's Danielle [our younger daughter]? Are your parents doing okay? Do they need anything? Don't hesitate to call." He didn't want to portray himself as a nice guy, is all. He had a reputation as a pit bull, and he wanted to maintain that.

The later I got into my career, the more it became my responsibility to stand toe-to-toe with him. I was the guy the younger players looked to on how to handle difficult situations—the person who'd tell George to get out, the person to talk to the manager if there was an issue, or talk to George. In the early part of my career, that was Thurman. I wasn't Thurman. He was more outspoken and forceful. Generally, I was more quiet.

But on a day-to-day basis, I didn't have to be an asshole. Part of that was because the character of the ballplayers had changed over time. The players coming up in the eighties weren't as boisterous and crazy as we were. There were fewer

Sparky Lyles and Lou Piniellas. In the seventies we couldn't wait for the shit to hit the fan, because it was fun to watch. In the eighties the players were meeker. They didn't yell or fight with the manager as much. They still played the game, but I'm referring to their demeanor. They didn't want to get into fights. Maybe they realized there was no upside in it.

———

George named Willie and me co-captains prior to the 1986 season. Obviously, it was a tremendous honor. Since the passing of Lou Gehrig, no Yankee had been captain until Thurman. After Thurman passed, it was unclear if there would ever be one again. After all, the post was left vacant for decades after Gehrig. In '82, George had made Nettles captain. Then he was traded to San Diego. The funny thing was, Graig and Thurman both fought a lot with George. Not like that clubhouse jawing—this was real, tense stuff. Thurman fought over some contractual stuff and at one point asked for a trade. Nettles and George said a lot of nasty stuff about each other in the papers. Graig leveled a lot of that in his book, *Balls*, which precipitated his trade away from the team.

Willie and I met with George during spring training that year, and George outlined what he thought the role of captain should be. He thought we should be a voice for the players, to speak up about any issues and represent them if anything came up. Willie and I were cut from a different cloth from Thurman and Graig. We didn't have any simmering feuds with management. Sure, George and I would exchange barbs in the clubhouse, but that was just good sport. Especially later in my career, he and I got along well and had a special friendship. (Don't forget the stew.) And as for Willie, he was as low-maintenance as it got—stoic, quiet, the type of ballplayer who just professionally went about his business every single day. He never created a problem and largely kept to himself. He wasn't the type of guy who would verbally spar with George in the clubhouse. There was no riling Willie. He was impressively levelheaded.

In actuality, though, there were more ass-chewings from George throughout the eighties than we experienced in the late seventies. Between Thurman, Reggie, and Billy, George had plenty of people to fight with in those years. Plus, we were really good. He didn't need to do as much motivating. In the eighties we weren't as good. George, though, expected a championship every year. Or at least he acted like he did.

The thing about those earlier teams was we were blessed with so many players who would go on to be remembered as Yankees legends. For whatever reason, there were fewer of those guys in the eighties. But that shouldn't be confused with saying we didn't have some good players—we certainly did in some certain spots.

Take our outfield starting in 1985, which added Rickey Henderson to join Dave Winfield. Those two guys were such incredible defenders we probably could've played with just two outfielders. Rickey didn't have much of an arm, but that was no matter—he caught near every damn ball. He made the hard plays look easy. And if a play looked hard for him, it meant nobody else in baseball would've caught it.

Those guys were already stars before they came to New York, but when you actually get to see them for 162 games, you get to fully appreciate just how talented they are. Rickey for so long was a thorn in our butt when he played for Oakland—he stole at least 100 bases three times for them—and you got to see just how fast the son of a gun was when you saw him every day.

Some people have said over the years that Rickey was quirky or difficult to deal with, and in the broadest strokes that might've been true. He had to be coddled a little bit. Some guys you could yell at and tell them to get their shit together. He was more the type that needed to be patted on the butt. But do you think that was a problem? No. As our teams in '77 and '78 showed, if you played the game the right way, that's what mattered. And he sure did.

As for Winfield, wow, was he special. The guy was probably a Hall of Famer before he got to New York. Then he got to New York and had a second Hall of Fame career with us. People like to talk about five-tool players all the time. Those are the guys who can do everything. But as much as people use the term, it's rarely actually true. Winfield was one of those rare players. He was one of those guys who were simply fun to watch play. He did everything right. He did it with ease. And he was a damn good ballplayer.

But as a veteran, I really paid closest attention to the guys who I could tell would wear the uniform for a long time. If you can have an impact on somebody like that, you can sit back and take pride in what they're doing long after you're done playing.

Take Don Mattingly. He first came up in '82 as a twenty-one-year-old. He would watch how I interacted with George and with other teammates, much the same way I observed Thurman and Lou and Graig. The way someone goes about his work tells you a lot about the individual. Donny worked so damn hard, he may have given himself the bad back that ended his career. The guy took five thousand swings per day.

I wanted to shake him and say, "Donny, the good Lord gave you the ability to hit .300 or .350. You don't need to kill yourself to hit .301 or .351."

But he just kept working. He wanted to get that one more hit. That's how he was. If you watched Willie, Reggie, Thurman, or Lou take batting practice, they'd go out and take their cuts. If they stepped in, *thwack,* line drive, *thwack,* line drive, five times in a row. They knew they were good. They'd drop their bat on the ground and walk off.

With guys like Donny and even today, if you tell a batter he can hit for ten minutes, he'll hit for ten minutes. If you tell him he can take fifty swings, he'll take his fifty and ask for twenty-five more. If Willie hit five balls on the nose, he was good. I think not overpracticing extended the careers of some of those guys. It's not that they didn't work hard, it's that they worked smart. They'd take more cuts if they needed to, but they wouldn't do it just for the sake of doing so.

———

Because I was a pitcher, it was naturally easier for me to have an impact on other pitchers. The irony of the Sparky trade is that we traded away my mentor for somebody who I'd eventually get to look after. Connecting with Dave Righetti was no accident. When we traded for him, the team told me they were going to put his locker next to mine so I could give him pointers. They said he was a left-hander with great stuff but could get a little wild.

Around the same time, I met Dave's father, Leo Righetti. Mr. Leo was a longtime minor leaguer in the Yankees organization. He never made the big leagues, but he was a fine ballplayer by all accounts and understood the game. He approached me and told me the same thing. "I'd like for you to do me a favor. I want you to keep an eye on Dave. He's got talent; he's just got to harness it."

Now, this didn't require me telling him to sit down and listen. I mostly observed how he acted and pitched, and gave him advice, much the way guys had done for me. He first had a cup of coffee in the bigs as a twenty-year-old in '79, then pitched incredibly well in the strike-shortened '81 season, when he won Rookie of the Year. The thing about Dave was that while he had a tremendous arm, he could lose his control. In '82 he led the league with 108 walks. To start the '82 season he had a couple of rough outings. And after each one, he bravely faced the reporters, who were all over him. He never shied away. But I could see that he was down and needed some counseling.

"Dave, do you think you can pitch here?"

"Yeah."

"Well, how did you get here, anyway?"

"What?"

"Did you get here because you were a finesse pitcher?"

"No, I'm a power pitcher," he said.

"Why don't you pitch that way? That's not what you've been doing. At least if they hit you, they're hitting your best stuff."

All I was telling him was to be himself. He for some reason had gotten the impression that because he was in the majors, he had to start developing more pitches, throwing more changeups and curveballs. He had a great fastball and a mean slider. But he wasn't using them as much as he should have been. He wasn't going to reach his potential by throwing junk. And all I had to do was remind him why he got to the big leagues in the first place.

When Dave really became special, though, was as a closer. Goose left us to sign with San Diego after '83, leaving us a gaping hole at the back of the bullpen. For so long, that was something we'd never had to worry about. My entire career we'd had two of the best ever in Sparky and Goose. Now, for the first time in a long while, the team didn't have an obvious answer for who to put back there. It came down to two options: me or Dave.

At first they wanted me to do it. I had experience relieving sporadically in the past and had done it successfully in the minors, so there wasn't much doubt I could thrive in the role. But I felt like it was a little too late for me. Was it worth turning me into a closer when nobody was sure how many years I had left? It's possible at one time that might have been best for my career. I may have lasted longer if I became a full-time closer. But I was ultimately concerned with what was best for the Yankees. And I looked at Dave, who was just twenty-five, and saw somebody who might be able to close for the next decade.

So when George called me that off-season, that's what I told him. I suggested that it should come from me, because Dave might be more open to the idea. It also might help Dave because he tended to tire late in the season and needed to be protected either by leaving games early or by skipping a start here and there. His arm might be best suited for the closer role, I thought. Dave embraced the idea completely and set a major-league record at the time with forty-six saves in 1986.

The way George handled that—calling me, involving me

in the decision—says a lot about him. Not long before, he was screaming and hollering that he wanted me out. We had gone from one end of the spectrum to the other. It was the same way with Billy; it's something they had in common. In fact, it wouldn't be a stretch to say they feuded so much not because they were so different but because they were so similar. They treated and trusted people similarly. Once you earned their respect, you had it. You don't have to worry about that again. They might pick on you here and there, but that's good-natured and really just letting you know they haven't forgotten about you. Once you've earned their respect, these guys would do anything for you. And it made us a better team.

Later I would have a similar relationship with pitcher Al Leiter. He would go on to have his best seasons elsewhere, with the Marlins and then across town with the Mets, but it was especially rewarding for me to watch Al and Dave because they reminded me a lot of myself as a pitcher. As people, they were both riots. Left-handers have the reputation of being kind of quirky oddballs. They were like that, young guys in New York City. Single, drinking, carousing. And all of a sudden I was the old guy marveling at their ability, the way Sparky would turn to Tidrow and say, "I created a monster out of Gator." I'd get that same feeling looking at them. Even if I had the same ability, you can't watch yourself pitch. So I would work with them and watch them snap off a breaking ball and think to myself, *Does the ball look like that coming out of my hand? Wow.*

———

After I retired, I gave something special to Dave: my locker. But it wasn't really *mine*. It was a locker in the corner of the clubhouse—corner lockers were the biggest—and it was passed down to and from a number of people I was close to. To give you a picture of our clubhouse, this was on the opposite side of the bathrooms, about ten feet from the entrance.

By the time I became a big leaguer, Sparky had that corner locker. In order down the wall, the adjacent lockers belonged to Tidrow, me, Yogi, then Elston Howard. I was pretty lucky, right? The two guys who mentored me right there, and Yogi Berra on the other side.

When Sparky was traded, that locker went to Graig Nettles. And since we acquired Dave and they wanted me to work with him, they had put him next to me. So it was Graig in the corner, then Dave, then me. Nettles left after '83, and I flipped over to the corner spot, but Dave was still next to me but on the other side. I stayed there until I left, after which I gave it to Dave. Then he gave it to Mattingly.

It's a small thing, but it always stood out to me as a symbol of something we passed on. These were all guys who are remembered as Yankees, and to us it was a spot of honor. And lockers obviously have a famous place in Yankees lore, the way Thurman's locker always stayed around in memory of him.

————

During the mid-eighties we had plenty of strong players and fairly good teams. But the teams were never complete. We were always lacking one thing or another. When we could score, we lacked pitching depth. When we had a deep rotation, we couldn't hit. When we moved Dave Righetti to the bullpen, we had another great closer, but then all of a sudden we didn't have a strong starter to take his spot. All in all, it produced a different atmosphere from that of our best teams. Even when we had all the pieces, not everybody would produce on a given day. But we all compensated for one another—different days, different heroes—to win ball games. Without a complete ball club, it doesn't go as smoothly.

And the years we didn't have Billy as manager—Billy was back with us in '83 and '85—the games didn't have the same type of fireworks. For all the issues between Billy, George, and some of the players, Billy was a world-class manager who could squeeze every single win out of a team, because the guys played so damn hard for him. That was the story of his managerial career in Minnesota, Detroit, Texas, and Oakland too. He often took over rosters that didn't have much talent or previous success and turned them into winners.

Now, it wasn't always as crazy when Billy was managing us again in '83, but there was one time that became like nothing anybody had ever seen before. It's so famous it only needs three words for any baseball fan to know what I'm talking about: Pine Tar Game. This was one game played on two days over the course of nearly a month and involved two controversial decisions that drove pretty much everyone completely mad.

Most of the wildest stuff during these years happened against Boston or Kansas City. This time, it was the Royals. We led 4–3 in the top of the ninth. There were two outs and they had a runner on first. Goose Gossage was on the mound, George Brett was at the plate. Brett got a hold of one, a deep towering shot over the right-field wall in Yankee Stadium, 5–4 Royals . . . until Billy came out of the dugout. There wasn't any hesitation: He knew beforehand what he was doing because Billy and some of the savvy guys in our dugout had an eye for things like this. The pine tar on Brett's bat, Billy argued—and Billy was never one to be polite or reserved in his disputes—exceeded what was allowed in the rules. The ump measured it and deemed Billy correct. He pointed to the Royals dugout: You're out. Brett was livid. I saw a lot of angry guys on the diamond. Brett stormed out of the dugout. His face looked like it was turning purple. I'm surprised he didn't deck someone. But that was the third out, and the ball game was over.

We won 4–3 . . . until we didn't. The Royals protested the game to the league offices, and they won the protest. That's not all: Brett was also ejected for arguing with the umps, as was Dick Howser from our side. And the game wasn't over. We still had a chance to tie it or win it in the bottom of the ninth. A game that began on July 24 had to be finished on August 18, without the guy at the center of what became one of baseball's all-time fiascos.

So the game resumed in August. That in part had to do with Billy, who protested the league's decision about the protest. He wanted to rub everyone's noses in how ridiculous this had become. So he made the conclusion of the game even more ridiculous. I was at the center of his shenanigans: He put me in the outfield. It was actually a thrill for me—I always said I thought I could play the outfield well because I was pretty fast and good at tracking down balls. And now I was going to get the chance to play in centerfield at Yankee Stadium. He also put Don Mattingly in at second base. Me in the outfield and Don Mattingly, a lefty, at second. Unfortunately, we had just one out to get against the Royals, and it was a strikeout. Neither Don nor I got the ball.

We went down 1-2-3 in the bottom of the ninth and lost the game 5–4. But it's a story that lives on in baseball history because of how absurd it became. It was also quintessential Billy Martin: His smarts, craziness, and stubbornness all wrapped up into one bizarre game.

Managers like Gene Michael, Bob Lemon, and Clyde King were great for morale, but we didn't have as much fun. Watching the skirmishes between Billy and George was entertaining. It was a reason to wake up in the morning and get to the ballpark early. Without that, the New York Yankees were just another ball club. Without Billy, George didn't have anybody to ride. In some years that was a plus—as I said, I do not believe we would have won the World Series in '78 without Lemon's steady hand and cool demeanor. These guys were very good managers. They were just different from Billy. As the years passed and I became one of the few guys left from the championship teams, that Billy energy was something I missed.

The toughest thing for me personally was what happened during Yogi's tenure as manager. He was hired to replace Billy in '84, and we had quite a decent season, with eighty-seven wins. But it was a difficult situation. On the one hand, George loved having a Hall of Famer and a World Series winner managing the team. On the other hand, it was hell being a manager for George. He'd get the players he wanted, insist on the players he wanted to play or sit on the bench, and want the lineup filled out a certain way. And he tortured Yogi over many of his decisions, the same way he tortured Billy.

Yogi, of course, had been one of our coaches before that. He was a baseball rat who had an unending knowledge of the game. As a coach, he was chummy with me and the guys. You'd find him lounging around, often in his underwear or less, having a drink, a smoke, or a chew. Ask him anything about baseball, and he always had an answer. But as a coach, he didn't have to deal with any pressure from George. Once he was a manager, it was another story.

For me, seeing him as a manager was naturally rewarding. Our lockers had been next to each other, and we had grown close. He was beloved by everyone, not just me, because he was such a complete human being—tough, goofy, passionate, silly, and caring too. He wasn't just good to me as a ballplayer. As we grew closer he took the time and interest to get to know my family. It's one of the great marks of Yogi, and the same was true of George. They both cared enough to develop a genuine relationship with my family as well as with me.

Yogi was smart enough to know that if you sign up to manage for George Steinbrenner, there's a good chance it's not going to last for long. The same is true for any sports team really, but managing under George was an extreme example. Heck, Billy had to leave midway through the season, after winning the World Series! So Yogi didn't have any delusions about being the manager forever.

But the way he was fired was hard for me to stomach. We were sixteen games into the '85 season, in Chicago, when George made the decision. First of all, that's way too early in the season to make a change. But the worst thing was that George didn't call Yogi to tell him the news, or deliver it face-to-face. Someone else in the front office informed Yogi. The veteran guys like me and Willie, who knew Yogi well, we were pissed.

The way Yogi responded to his firing said a lot about his character. After learning he was fired in Chicago, Yogi took the team bus with us back to the airport! To him it made perfect sense. He had to get to the airport—it's not like he was going to stay in Chicago. But I doubt you'll see many people in his position so damn practical that, even while seething in anger, they'd hop on the team bus with all the players like that.

Another aspect of Yogi, which played out over time, was his unwavering commitment to principle. You could also call it stubbornness. When he said something, when he believed something, that's the way it was. As a player and in life, Yogi didn't do anything halfheartedly. So when he said that because of what Mr. Steinbrenner did, he wasn't going to return to Yankee Stadium again, even to take part in Old Timers' Day, that's how it was going to be. And for fourteen years the Yankees didn't see him again. For someone like Yogi, that's a damn eternity, because every fiber of his being itched to be down at spring training camp, on a baseball field, watching, teaching, and taking part in the action. It was hell for him being away. But he believed there was a right way and a wrong way to treat people, and he wanted to make his point.

———————

As I got deeper into my career, I began to be appreciated more for something that was easy to overlook earlier in my career: my fielding. I was always good at fielding—it came naturally to me. I had good hands and good reaction skills. In high school I excelled in track and field, and that speed helped me develop a certain quickness on the mound. It's something that I had always worked on during spring training. After practice, two or three times per week, I'd have a coach hit me fifty or more ground balls on the back fields. They wouldn't tell me which way they were going to hit it, because it was all reaction skills. Ground balls, bunts, choppers, line drives. Left side, right side, right at me.

And my pitching mechanics always tended to put me in an ideal fielding position. Because I threw the ball right over the top—from 12 to 6 on a clock, so to speak—my momentum carried me straight forward toward home plate. Other power pitchers, like Goose or Nolan Ryan, didn't throw straight over the top. They threw with more of a three-quarters motion. Which meant they more or less spun to one side. There's nothing wrong with that—those are two of the greatest pitchers of all time. It just so happened that my delivery allowed me to be a better fielder. Watch a slow-motion film of me throwing, and you'll notice I have a hop right at the end of my delivery. By the time I landed with both feet on the ground, my feet were spread apart in ready position, just like an infielder's.

I never drew accolades for my fielding earlier in my career. It's just something that people didn't really notice. I didn't win the first of my Gold Gloves until 1982, when I was thirty-two years old. I won the award for the next four seasons after that, too.

But as I grew older I also changed as a pitcher. Once I hit my mid-thirties—and this is true for every pitcher, really—I started to lose some of the zip off my fastball. That didn't mean all of a sudden I was incapable of throwing the ball ninety-six miles per hour. It meant I just couldn't do it as frequently. In 1978, when I was twenty-seven, I could throw it as hard as I wanted for 130 pitches per night. Later in my career, I might only be able to dial it up that hard a few dozen times a game.

It required me to become smarter as a pitcher, which is why I was still able to have some great seasons in the mid-eighties. Same was true of Catfish: He had some great seasons toward the end of his career. He joked that he'd be able to get guys out if he was throwing eighty miles per hour. It had to do with the way he set up batters, located his pitches, and induced weak contact. In time, I learned to do the same.

It wasn't always easy. My body ached more as I got older. In 1984 I had a 10-11 record with a 4.51 ERA, and I went on the disabled list for the first time in my career. Still, playing in more than two hundred games without going on the DL was quite a feat, something I attribute to either luck or maybe not overworking my arm, especially during the winter. These changes didn't mean all of a sudden I became some sort of junk pitcher. I mixed in the occasional curveball and changeup, but I was still mostly a fastball and slider pitcher.

The difference was learning how to pitch intelligently and get outs even without blowing the ball past everybody. When I needed to, I could sling one with some oomph to get a big out. Those pitches actually became more effective, because if I'm throwing ninety-two, ninety-two, ninety-two, then whiz one at ninety-six, they don't have much of a chance at hitting it.

Take my 1985 season. Some people wondered if I was over the hill with the injury and the struggles I had in '84. That year I went 22-6 with a 3.27 ERA and finished second in the Cy Young voting. And although my résumé lists only four All-Star Games ('78, '79, '82, '83), I was invited in '85 as well but chose not to go. That was part of becoming older—Billy preferred that I not go so I'd have some extra days to rest my arm. I was happy to do so. The baseball season is long, and a few days off to spend with Bonnie and the kids was a rare treat.

The point about that 1985 year, though, is how different it looked from my other strong seasons. In '78 I struck out 248 guys. In '79, I struck out 201. In '85, I struck out only 143 despite throwing more innings (259) than I did in any season other than '78. That was the lowest strikeout rate of my career but one of my best seasons. I walked opposing batters at the lowest rate of my career and generally succeeded at inducing weak contact. And I think that speaks to why my fielding got noticed more. There isn't as much fielding when so many at-bats end in a strikeout. When more balls were put in play, I had more of a chance to display my fielding abilities.

We won ninety-seven games in 1985, falling just two short of Toronto in a year when Don Mattingly won the MVP. We didn't make the playoffs again in my last years. Which is why to me those years are much more about the people. Showing the younger players how to handle George, teaching them about the game, going out there on a day-to-day basis and doing my best to set an example about the right way to play ball. I never knew exactly when my career would end, but most of all I wanted to retire with my family financially secure. Which, for a time, was sadly uncertain.

12

BECOMING A MONUMENT

I never let the night life, city life, or any other type of New York City shenanigans athletes get into interfere with what I was trying to do. When we were at home, a big night was having a beer in the clubhouse, or stopping on the way home for a bite and a drink with Catfish or one of the other players at the TGI Fridays on Route 4. More often than not I was just eager to get home to heat up whatever Bonnie had left me for dinner. On the road, the most I ever spent was on my room service bill up in Toronto, because there was a Trader Vic's in the hotel and I couldn't get enough of that food. So I was pretty low-maintenance. When I was a kid we never had much money, but we were happy. With my earnings as a Yankee, I was mainly concerned with buying a nice piece of land in Lafayette for our family, a pension, and lifelong security.

Given that, I was shocked, heartbroken, and troubled to discover I was on the verge of bankruptcy before the start of the 1984 season. When I was a free agent after the 1981 season, I signed a four-year deal for $3.95 million. That was quite a bit of money at the time, and I thought it might be the last contract I would sign. It was more than enough for me. But without my knowledge, most of it vanished. It's not something I have spoken about much. I didn't want to burden my teammates with a personal problem. It wasn't because I was boozing, gambling, or buying stupid shit. Really, it was a lesson about putting too much trust in one person.

My agent and lawyer handled my investments and such for my company, Ron Guidry Enterprises. He wasn't just my lawyer and agent, though. He was a lifelong friend, someone who I knew growing up and played ball with in Lafayette. I gave him power of attorney because I understand with some business things you need to act at the snap of a finger. But it turned out, as time went on, that he was signing my name on things I'd never approved. Many of the deals or investments I never even knew about. Creditors and debtors don't care who signed. So I had a giant mess to clean up.

Eventually, when he told us what was going on, we parted ways. But the damage was done. And he had told us about a few of the things going on, so I wasn't blameless. In my eyes, if I lost ten dollars, three dollars of it was my fault and seven dollars was his. There was a time around Lafayette earlier in my career when industry was booming. When the oil companies are doing well, so is Lafayette. But when the recession hit, it was clear he had overextended himself. He was involved in too many things, and some of them he had put my name on.

There was nothing to do but take a sober look at everything I had and face the music. I threatened to file for bankruptcy—some people advised that. It would've been the easiest thing to do. But if you do that, they seize all of your assets. I didn't want to lose what I had—the beautiful piece of land in Lafayette, which I still have today. I laid all my problems out on a table with a new attorney, and we went one by one to the various people and businesses I learned I owed money to and worked out deals.

And in the grand scheme of things I was still in good shape. I wasn't out on the street starting over again. I had a job; I was making good money. Outside of the business, I had saved money. So we got everybody on the debt list to agree to what I was offering them. If I owed them one dollar, I'd give them fifty or sixty cents. It worked for everybody, because if I declared bankruptcy, they would've gotten less. They also knew their claims were on shaky grounds, because I hadn't signed the deals. They were done behind my back, without my knowledge. If they didn't take my offer, I could've fought to pay them nothing.

But we went to court, the judge agreed, the creditors agreed, and the case was closed. I was clear. I lost a lot of what I had earned, but they couldn't come after me again. I didn't want to be walking around owing people money. That's something George told me to avoid, and he was right. And I still had what mattered—the house, my long-term security, and a job. I was also able to play longer than I expected. I didn't keep playing because of the money, but I was essentially as good in 1985 as I was in my prime. There was no sense in hanging up my spikes yet.

It's not something I'm proud to have gone through, because it was difficult for both me and the family. And my family was and always has been more important to me than what happened on the field. But we tackled it. After that, I gave Bonnie power of attorney so it could never happen again.

———

Eventually, however, my age and all the innings I threw caught up to me. It's an inevitability in this game. But you never know how or exactly when it will happen. My final big-league game came in 1988. In '86, I was solid if not spectacular, with a 3.98 ERA in thirty starts and a 9-12 record. The next year, '87, I had a 3.67 ERA but made it into only twenty-two games. In 1988, that number declined to twelve.

The end really came during the spring of '89, when I had surgery on a bone spur in my elbow. But it wasn't just the injury—I could've come back, and I actually had the best spring training of my career before I got hurt, not that I ever put much stock in spring performance. Still, it showed I had gas left in the tank. It also had to do with our new manager.

Before the '89 season we hired Dallas Green, who previously had some success managing the Phillies. But we would never have got along had I actually played for him. I'm pretty sure he didn't want me there for some reason, but that wasn't his call.

At the beginning of spring training, he called a meeting and something happened. You could say we got off on the wrong foot. He was standing right at the entrance to where you go to the lavatories and showers, and I was sitting nearby on a bench in front of my locker. As he started to address the team, he began walking. He stepped, hard, on my foot. I got up to move my feet, but I was rather shocked. I felt that he was in the wrong and should've acknowledged it and apologized in some sort of way. He never said he was sorry or anything, and just kept talking as if nothing had happened.

It wasn't just that, though. It was *what* he was saying. *"This is what I want done. I want it done this way."* I was taken aback. I had dealt with plenty of managers, got on differently with all of them, but none of them spoke in the way that he was talking. They'd say, *"This is what we'd like to accomplish. We'd like to work on this. We'd like to get better at this."* It was that "I" versus "we." It grated on me, and I thought it said a lot about how he viewed us and the team.

So the next day, I knew Dallas was gonna give us another talk. But beforehand, I looked across the locker room and Don Mattingly had the locker directly across from mine. He had a bunch of bats, and one was cast off to the side.

"Hey, Donnie, that bat that's by itself. You doin' anything with it?"

"Nope."

"Mind if I borrow it for a minute?"

"Sure."

So I sat down with it and sat in front of my locker, just as I had the day before. But this time I had the bat in my hand. Dallas comes in and gets ready to start talking again. I leaned over and kind of tapped it a couple times against the ground. He looked at me.

"What the hell do you think you're doing?"

"If you walk on my feet again this morning," I said, "I swear to God I'll break your frickin' ankle."

Of course, he got pissed. After the meeting, he sent one of our coaches to tell me to go meet with him in his office. He was cursing, ranting and raving, because I had showed him up in front of everybody else. I told him he was the one who started it and who didn't treat me with common decency. I don't mean to attack the man's character here; other people have spoken highly of him. This was just my experience. It was just clear it was never gonna work between us. (And, it's worth noting, he was fired after less than a full season.)

After some rehab, I came back from the arm surgery and felt physically fine. There was no question that I wasn't my former self. But I thought I was at maybe 85 percent—which still made for a viable starter, especially on a team that was often hurting for starting pitchers. But after the surgery the Yankees had me pitching in Double-A to prove my health, endurance, and effectiveness. And at a certain point, it just felt like I was spinning my wheels. Why go through all of this?

I had made all the money I needed to make. I had a beautiful house and family in Lafayette. I was eager to spend more time there. I loved the game, but at the same time I knew I wouldn't miss it. I was ready to begin a new life, from a different perspective. It made me happy to see Dave Righetti in my former locker, in the corner of the clubhouse, and players like Don Mattingly, knowing the Yankees tradition would carry on.

Being away from guys like that would be the hardest part, I knew. In the clubhouse, I had twenty-four brothers. I knew I would miss them. Still, I wouldn't miss my arm aching and hearing the voices of my kids over the phone as they grew up. Jamie was twelve already. My son Brandon was nine, and Danielle, our daughter, was four. I had an exciting new career ahead of me as a full-time father.

I didn't make a big show of it when I retired in July of '89. I met with reporters at Yankee Stadium, and we reminisced about my '78 season, the eighteen-strikeout game, and the craziness of what was now a decade earlier, although still fresh in my mind. I just wanted a chance to say good-bye, and wanted to do it alongside Bonnie and my three kids, who all joined me that day. It wasn't easy—baseball and hunting were the only two things I knew anything about, I told the reporters. But I didn't see myself as losing baseball. I was just about to see it from a new lens.

———

From time to time I'm asked whether I'm disappointed not to have made the Hall of Fame. The answer is no. I didn't need that. The game had given me so much. Bonnie and I had moved from the little apartment we shared behind my parents' place to a beautiful house in Lafayette, where we grew up. It was the house we raised our children in, and now it's home to our grandchildren. Maybe if I'd made myself miserable and won a few more games, or notched a few end-of-career saves in the bullpen, I would have made a better case for the hall. But I won 170 and lost 91. I was proud of my achievements. I never regretted retiring when I did.

What really made me tear up was having my number, 49, retired in 2003. It was quite a gesture by Mr. Steinbrenner. He and I had grown close during my later years as a Yankee, but our relationship really became something special when I was no longer a player. Then we could sit and talk as equals. He would eat my rabbit stew, put his arm around me, and we'd watch the current players together. I was choked up by his decision to put me out in Monument Park alongside the names of people like Reggie, Yogi, Billy, Thurman, Don Mattingly, Whitey Ford, Roger Maris, Mickey Mantle, Joe DiMaggio, Lou Gehrig, and Babe Ruth.

I was always cognizant of the fact that when I retired, I did so quietly. I essentially said, "I'm going home." To me, this moment was the chance to properly thank the Yankees fans for everything they meant to me, everything they did for me, and everything they said to me over the years. They would always ask me if I could hear them when I was on the mound. I didn't hear anyone in particular, but I could hear the roar. It was a distant thunder. It lifted me up to be the best that I could. It always made me proud to perform at Yankee Stadium. There are a lot of things at work when you talk about home-field advantage: The grounds crew can cut the grass in a certain way that fits your style, and you know the dimensions of the ballpark down to the inch. But pitching in front of Yankee Stadium fans is different than pitching in front of any other fans. They actually made me better than I probably made myself. I wanted to thank them for that.

That day, August 23, I went to Yankee Stadium not knowing quite what to expect. Bonnie knew what was going on. She had coordinated the event with the Yankees without my knowledge. I don't know how she did it, but it made it even more special. I thought they were simply honoring me, and then, with a host of Yankees legends like Yogi and Whitey on the field, they revealed my bronze plaque. I felt a surge of emotion like no other. It was an incredible acknowledgment by George and the Yankees of what I had done. Who needs the Hall of Fame when your plaque lives out in Monument Park alongside the *greatest* players for the *greatest* team in history, so many of the legends of all time?

———

I grew up idolizing Roger Maris and Mickey Mantle. Maris's sixty-one-home-run season, and the home-run chase between Mantle and Maris in 1961, took place right as I was falling in love with the game. Old Timers' Days had come and passed, and I had never introduced myself to Maris. I wanted to, badly. But Roger always seemed like a very private person.

We were in the clubhouse before the game, the old-timers talking to the current players. I leaned forward in my chair, staring at him. "Who are you looking at?" asked Mickey, seated next to me.

"I'm looking at Roger."

"You've never met him?"

"No," I said. "I would love to, but I didn't want to bother him."

"*Hey, Rog,*" Mickey called across the clubhouse. "Come over here a second. This young man here would like to say hello."

I stood up and shook Maris's hand. "Mr. Maris, it's very nice to meet you."

"Ron," he replied, "I'm so glad. I've been dying to meet you, but I didn't want to bother you."

Then we sat down and talked baseball. I asked him about the home-run chase and playing on those great Yankees teams of the sixties. And he wanted to know about *me*. I had won the Cy Young by this point and was an established player. Still, it was quite the feeling. Roger Maris wanted to ask me about my pitching? How I threw my slider?

That in a nutshell is why I loved Old Timers' Day so much. As soon as the schedule came out, I'd look at the calendar to circle whatever day it was. Because Yogi had his locker next to mine, with Elston Howard next to him, our side of the clubhouse was stacked. We'd have Mickey and Whitey Ford alongside us. Then I'd watch the rest of Yankees royalty file in. Joe DiMaggio. Vic Raschi. Eddie Lopat. Mantle. Maris. I'd be at the park by 8 A.M. just so I didn't miss a thing.

For a player, it's a surreal feeling. I'd seen so many of the World Series games on television. I had read about these guys, watched them, heard about them. Then, suddenly, there they were, talking to me, telling me what it was like. And they wanted to know about me, what it was like playing for George and Billy.

"Hey, Whitey," Mickey hollered across the clubhouse. "How good do you think we would've been if we had this guy?"

"I don't know," Whitey replied. "I don't think I would've been as good pitching from the number two spot."

They went out of their way to forge a relationship with me and the others, in a way that gave me goose bumps. Mickey and Whitey could spin a great story, because they didn't hold anything back. They came from that generation that was just brutally honest. They did what they did and didn't try to cover anything up. I'm not breaking any news here by saying those teams were famous for carousing.

The one thing that stood out to me most was how well those guys got along. They seemed to have a great camaraderie. It helped me to understand how they won so much. They might have been fierce competitors on the field, but they were good friends off the field. Good ballplayers can win games, but it takes a certain chemistry to win as much as they did. It's why we won, the fighting and the camaraderie.

Me and a few other people pushed to have the players' wives involved. I believe it started with Mrs. Arlene Howard, when Elston passed away. All the families had grown so close that it was a shame to not have them there. They had to go through so much on their own when we were off playing that I felt they never got enough appreciation. So while Thurman couldn't be there, his memories live on when Diana, his wife, comes. Same with Jill Martin after Billy passed; Helen Hunter, Catfish's wife; and Kay Murcer, Bobby's wife—to name a few.

The Yankees are obviously fortunate to have more of these legends and Hall of Famers than any team in the world. But the club, especially under George, always had a special understanding of its history. The organization always cherished and embraced it. It was fun for the fans, as well as for the players.

George enjoyed Old Timers' Day. He understood that when he acquired the team, he acquired its history too.

Once I retired, it gave me something to look forward to. Hearing your name called once again, watching the fans cheer for you again, it's quite a thrill.

It also gave me an opportunity to grow closer with some of the all-time greats who I had gotten to know as a player. Mickey and Whitey started holding a fantasy camp down in Florida every year, where people pay to play ball for a week, with coaching and instruction. When I retired, they invited me to be one of the coaches.

It quickly became clear that I wouldn't have any trouble staying close to the Yankees after I retired. After my press conference, I was summoned to George's office.

"Gator," he said, "I'd still like to see you at spring training next year, working with the guys."

13

COACH GATOR

During spring training of '93, one of our coaches, Mark Connor, came up to me and said he'd like me to take a look at one of the team's young pitchers. Every February since I had retired, I had made the eleven-or-so-hour drive from Lafayette to Florida to participate in spring training. George's offer to serve as a guest instructor was a generous one. I enjoyed being around the game, putting on the Yankees uniform, and getting to watch the young players. The team, I think, benefited too from having somebody around who'd had a lot of success in the major leagues, as the players got ready for the season.

I headed to one of the back fields that day to watch this young pitcher throw. He was just coming off surgery, so I didn't know what to expect. But I was curious because Mark told me the pitcher reminded him of someone, except he didn't tell me who. So I settled in to watch him throw. *Zip. Swoosh.* Despite recovering from surgery and being a skinny guy, the pitcher, Mariano Rivera, had incredible speed and movement on his ball.

"Who does he remind you of?" Mark asked after I had seen the kid throw his bullpen session.

"Well, if he was left-handed, he'd be me."

"Yeah, that's what everybody said."

I walked over to George with a message. The Yankees had left Mo unprotected in the 1992 expansion draft and were lucky that no team had claimed him. After seeing him pitch, I couldn't let them make the same mistake. "If you ever trade that kid right there," I said to George, pointing to Mo, "you'll never win any more championships."

The first couple years of spring training weren't that fun for me. Not because I was too close to my playing days but because I was one of the only steady guest instructors down there. I enjoyed leading the drills, getting to know the younger players, but there were fewer and fewer people I actually knew. This was at the height of the feud between Yogi and George. Whitey Ford would come, but he wasn't there every day. I just felt a little out of place.

When George called me during the winter before '92 spring training, he was a little surprised at our conversation.

"Gator, you planning on coming down again?"

"I'm not so sure, Mr. G."

"What?" he rasped. "What's the problem?"

"I'm having a great time, but I'm by myself," I told him. "Would you entertain the thought of asking somebody else to come?"

"Well, of course. But who?"

"Cat."

His voice boomed over the phone with excitement. "You think Catfish would come?" He was almost incredulous, and honored by the idea. I told him to give me a moment, that I'd call him back. I called Cat; his wife, Helen, answered the phone and put him on. I asked him if he'd be interested in being an instructor at spring training, and he laughed.

"Maybe," he said. "Tell George to call me." Half an hour later I got a call from Cat saying I'd see him in February.

It was Buck Showalter's first year as manager, and I think he was a little worried about me and Cat being there, maybe because we might overshadow him or because he feared we'd act as pipelines to George, giving reports about him. So on the first day he told me and Cat to go work with guys on the back fields, out of sight of the action. We did some drills with the players, worked on fundamentals, and so forth. Next day, we were in the back fields again. And every day afterward for the rest of the spring. About halfway through, we looked at each other and realized we hadn't been to the main field the entire time. It was as if we were intentionally being given nothing to do.

We weren't there to spy on or upstage Buck. But he didn't know that. It's nothing against Buck. He went on to have an incredible managerial career in New York, Arizona, Texas, and Baltimore. He has won AL Manager of the Year three times. But I took it personally, because I had recruited Cat-fish, a guy who's in the Hall of Fame and doesn't deserve to be treated like that. Of course, Cat being a class act, he didn't say shit about it. We just minded our own business and did our best to have a good time.

George got to doing some old-fashioned ass-chewing when he found out about it. He had asked if I'd be coming back again, and I told him it didn't go so well and that he shouldn't bother Cat by asking again. I can still hear his voice through the phone after I told him why. "*What?*" The following spring I don't think we went to the back fields once. And we all got along well with the other coaches, because it was clear we weren't there to spy on anybody. We were there to be a set of helping hands, a resource for the players. I was especially glad Cat became part of the fold, because in just a couple of years, he would be diagnosed with ALS. He passed away in 1999. I lost a great friend and kindred spirit, and the Yankees lost a great player and instructor.

Over the years, that coaches' room grew more and more crowded every spring with familiar faces. Goose retired after '94 and became a regular. The current players would walk by us and think we were having way too much fun. We enjoyed wearing the uniform and being around baseball for a month. And beyond the instructional aspects of our job, I think it was good for the current players to see that. The perceptive guys picked up on it.

I never ruled out the possibility of coaching. I never wanted to be a manager, but I thought in the right situation, I might enjoy the opportunity to coach the pitchers. I never angled for it, though, because the kids were still growing up and I wanted to spend as much time as I could back home. I would also only do it for the Yankees.

In the mid-2000s, Joe Torre felt me out. There were signs his longtime pitching coach, Mel Stottlemyre, might retire; Torre wanted to know if I'd consider replacing him. So for about a month, I shadowed Mel to see what the job entailed. I saw how he worked with certain guys. Who he would baby and who he would chew out. Who was serious and who was always cracking jokes. So much of the game had become about coaching by the numbers, using computerized charts and whatnot, and I knew I couldn't coach that way.

When Joe was looking for a new pitching coach after the 2005 season, I made that abundantly clear to him. I was eager to work with the pitchers and coach, but computerized baseball wasn't me. The Yankees front office wanted somebody who had those skills. But Joe loved the way I interacted with the guys during the spring and how they responded to me. He told me I wouldn't have to mess with the computers. He talked to George, and the old man was eager to have me back on board.

I knew going into it that I didn't want to be a long-termer. A few years at most. More than anything, I didn't want to grow old and never have tried coaching the newer players, to wonder "what if?" Bonnie agreed.

I'm not sure I would have done it if I weren't working for Joe Torre. Joe was an outstanding manager and an absolute pleasure to work for. We didn't win the World Series the two years I coached, 2006 and 2007, but we had some fun in the dugout. Don Mattingly, Lee Mazzilli, and I knew the balance between taking the game seriously and having fun. That's the thing about former players: We could be fiery as hell, but we never treated the game like a business, as is so often the case today. The clubhouse, the dugout, it shouldn't be stoic and 100 percent serious. And if you saw Joe Torre's face on television, you would see that he was quite a serious man. But we also made him laugh a lot.

During one game Joe made me go out to talk to Randy Johnson in the first inning. Now, Randy is one of the greatest pitchers to ever step onto a baseball field. He won 303 games and five Cy Young Awards and struck out 4,875 batters with a 3.29 career ERA. "The Big Unit," as he was known, threw hard as hell, and he was six foot ten. But RJ was hard to talk to. He didn't want much advice on his pitching and more generally wasn't perfectly cut out to handle the twenty-four-hour, in-your-face pressure of New York. Before playing a game for us, he got into some heat when he shoved a cameraman on the street.

During that game, I went out to talk to RJ in the first inning. The second inning didn't go much better, so Joe sent me out there to talk to him again. It wasn't fun, because I didn't have much to say to Randy, who was never in the mood to listen too much. So later in the game when Joe asked me to go out there a third time, I just exploded. "I don't wanna go out there and talk to that guy. If you want to, then just go do it."

So Joe went and did just that. He chatted with RJ on the mound, and when he came back he had this glazed, faraway look in his eyes. He turned to me and Mattingly on the bench and said, "He just doesn't get it, does he?" Joe always said he would've loved to have me pitch for him. I told him there was no way in hell I could've pitched for him.

"Why's that?"

"You come out to the mound too damn often."

"But if it had been you out there," Joe replied, "I wouldn't have to."

Even in the heat of battle, we could laugh at the little things. As I said before, catchers often make the best managers, and Joe was another example of that. He'd won four World Series and two more pennants with the Yankees.

What made Joe so great was his ability to keep the peace. He was the perfect manager at the perfect time. He had the innate ability to be calm when things got out of hand. It made him the opposite of Billy in many respects. Joe could balance everything, from the front office to the players to the day-to-day turmoil the team faces in the tabloids whenever the Yankees lose a game. He could compartmentalize extremely well.

He was also able to keep George in check better than any other manager I knew. George had mellowed over the years—by the time I was the pitching coach, he was in his mid-seventies—but the players in Joe Torre's clubhouse never had to face George the way we did. The way, when I was playing, George would come into the clubhouse screaming and hollering—that was mostly a thing of the past. Joe's calm demeanor put George at ease, and that put the guys on the team at ease. And that fit the personality of the players in those years. Joe's teams had some all-time Yankees greats, such as Derek Jeter, Bernie Williams, Jorge Posada, and Andy Pettitte, but they also weren't the types who would have told George to screw off if he got in their faces.

From 2008 to 2010, Joe went on to manage the Dodgers for three season. I'm not sure he would've asked me to join him as his pitching coach, though he might have. That never happened. I think I made it clear in previous conversations with him why. I stated it pretty simply: I could never wear Dodger blue. We had too many big games against them when I was a player, and I had worn only Yankees pinstripes my entire life. It wouldn't have been right.

The game was evolving quickly, too. The shift, more than anything, is one of the ways the game had changed between my time playing and coaching. It felt more like a business. Granted, there's a middle ground between the craziness I experienced as a player and the stoic, businesslike atmosphere today, but over the years the players had become far more clean-cut. As a coach, I'd walk onto the bus during a road trip and the first thing I noticed is that everybody had whipped out their phones or put their headphones on. Nobody talked to anybody. The magic of our Yankees teams was built on rowdy bus rides where there was no telling what would happen. Whatever shit went down, we had built a brotherhood on the buses, and if often felt like we were going to war together.

It built character. We tested one another. You could insult a man's dog, his house, his family, his accent, his schooling, his shoes, his hometown, his clothes, and none of it was taken personally. Nobody was overly sensitive about it, because it was all about whether or not you were quick enough and tough enough to dish it right back. It's why Lou Piniella was so beloved—nobody could talk shit like him.

Another thing that's different: Now when you see any team celebrate, with the champagne and whatnot, it's all so structured. They put these Visqueen plastic sheets all over the lockers and the floor, they have goggles for the players to protect their eyes from the spraying champagne, and it's this big to-do. We just soaked each other. It was all pure heat-of-the-moment stuff.

This shows just how informal it was: The first time my wife, Bonnie, met Yogi Berra, he was stark naked. Her words were he was "naked as a jaybird." We had just won the '77 World Series and we were all celebrating, going crazy, of course. He didn't have a care in the world. Why would he? We had just won the World frickin' Series.

So Yogi sauntered out, naked, to bring a bottle of champagne to his wife, Carmen. She just looked at Bonnie afterward and said, "Yep, that's Yogi." Naked as a jaybird.

———

Coaching, I learned, was a never-ending job. Mentally, it is much more taxing than playing. The only free time you've got is when you're home sleeping. There was a supermarket around the corner from where I lived in Manhattan where I could get a bite to eat, some coffee, and the paper. Other than that, I'd have to ask my son Brandon, who was living with us in the city, where anything was. As a player I had never lived in the city. And it's not like I had any time to explore. I was always doing something coaching-related. I'd drive to Yankee Stadium, get there by noon, and wouldn't leave for another twelve hours. That gets you back home after midnight, just in time to repeat the same thing the next day. It took a lot of organization, because before a game you're working with pitchers and going over things with Joe. After the game, you're assessing what happened in that night's game to get the reports ready for the following day.

I had two strengths as a pitching coach. The first was that as a pitcher, I always had a keen sense of the proper mechanics. People always told me that if you were to choose a soundtrack for my delivery, you'd choose ballet music. I always liked that. I didn't look like I was working hard, but everything had to be in perfect sync in order for a guy like me to throw as hard as I did. Take a guy like Goose. He threw in the upper nineties, but he was six foot three and weighed upward of two hundred pounds. He *looked* like he was throwing the ball hard. Same for Nolan Ryan. For me to throw ninety-five miles per hour, at just 150 pounds, my delivery had to be smooth and waste no motion, to generate as much power as my body would allow.

In an era that has turned the game into spray charts

and spreadsheets, the ballet has gotten lost. Oftentimes the numbers are just descriptive. They tell you how someone has played or performed on the field, and in greater depth than they ever did in my day. But sometimes to really understand *why* a pitcher is throwing well, or poorly, you need a keen eye for what he's doing physically. When I was playing, that was a skill we honed every day. I'd watch everybody, throwing for and against us, to study their mechanics. Now it seems like people watch the mechanics of the game less and miss picking up some of the nuances along the way.

Knowing the mechanics helped me as a pitching coach because I felt the most important thing was having a mental image of each pitcher and what he should look like. There's no such thing as perfect mechanics. No two of the best pitchers of all time wound up and threw the ball exactly alike. There are better practices than others, for sure, but what's most important is consistency. When things aren't working, it's usually because those mechanics are slipping and changing from pitch to pitch.

So the key was keeping a close eye on guys to let them know if something was off. For some guys, like Mariano Rivera, that might never be the case. He could throw four straight balls and then fire twenty straight strikes. Other guys, like Mike Mussina, were so good because they had a strong internal sense of when their mechanics were askew. Within one or two pitches, Mike could feel something was off and fix it. You see guys like Mussina who do that, and it's no wonder they had such incredible careers. Same goes for Roger Clemens, who at forty-four years of age pitched for us in the second half of 2007. He was one of the greatest pitchers ever, but what made him so inspiring to work with was that he was still obsessed over the little things, always trying to get better. "Gator, watch for this and make sure I do that," he'd tell me. To me, that was a sign of respect; even at his age, and with his illustrious career, he valued my insights.

The other thing I tried to do as a pitching coach was to learn the personalities of my pitchers. In many cases, figuring things out on the mound doesn't take a genius. The best advice I ever got from a pitching coach was from Art Fowler. When I first became a starter in 1977 he told me something amazingly simple: "If you can't throw strikes, you can't throw in the big leagues." That's it. It was so simple it was stupid. "What kind of pitching coach is this?" I said to myself. But then I sat down and thought about it. And it encapsulated everything I needed to know. Batters would never swing at my balls if I couldn't get them to swing and miss at my strikes. I could worry about throwing it this way or that way, on the corners and at their knees, but you can't beat yourself up out there. Other pitching coaches tried to give me more complicated advice that was never going to help me. I told them the best spot for them was in the corner; I'd figure things out on my own.

I'd study each of the pitchers to learn what worked best with him. Some responded better to going over film so they could see their delivery from several different angles. You compare what they're doing in the moment with what their form looked like when they were throwing their best. Others you could tweak right there on the mound in the middle of an inning. Some needed to go over stuff during bullpen sessions between starts. Some, like Randy Johnson, were best served by letting them deal with things by themselves.

I also had to learn what kind of attitude the pitchers

responded to. I never had to chew anybody out while I was a pitching coach, but some of the guys needed a different tone or approach. I could be stern, joking, philosophical—whatever they needed. Chien-Ming Wang, who had back-to-back nineteen-win seasons for us in '06 and '07, just needed to lighten up on the mound. So I could mess around with him. Same with Jaret Wright, who was so intense and would get so mad at himself, I had to struggle to keep him loose. I'd go out there, rub my mustache, and say, "So you've decided to make this damn game interesting, huh."

During moments like that I could hear a little bit of Thurman in myself, what I learned from him. He'd say things exactly like that to everybody on staff. If I helped my pitchers a fraction as much as Thurman helped me, I think I did my job.

In the years since that stint as pitching coach, I've come back to spring training every year and done the same thing: helped out, hung out, and observed. That annual trip to Florida is something I still look forward to—putting on the uniform, sitting in a clubhouse, and being near the game that gave so much to me. Some of the faces are still familiar. More seems to change every year. But it's such a darn interesting time in baseball—both specifically for the Yankees and across the entire league. A number of things have become completely different, both strategically and in the game's fundamentals.

The style of the game, from the way it's taught to the way it's managed and played, has completely changed over these last few decades. I don't care to lecture and say if it's better or worse. But the simple fact is that it's different. Let's start with the pitching. The starters today are nothing like they were in past eras. I don't mean that in terms of talent. Some of these guys are out of this world. But think about this: In 1978 I threw sixteen complete games. And another fifteen in '79. Then in '83 I threw twenty-one. Now, not a single pitcher in the last five years has reached even ten in a season. These days, some of the very best pitchers in the game go an entire season without pitching a game from beginning to end.

The reasons for this could fill a book. There's more science out there about pitch counts and not burning out a guy's arm. (Although it seems more and more pitchers need surgery anyway.) The main thing I want to get into, from my perspective as a player and a coach, is how this has stemmed from the increased specialization of players.

When I first got to the major leagues, and even the few years before that, is when the closer started to be a real specialized guy. Sparky was that guy for us. Then Goose. Oakland had Rollie Fingers. Mike Marshall won the Cy Young for the Dodgers in '74. But there wasn't really a setup guy. We had ten to eleven pitchers on the staff. Five starters, then five or six guys in the pen. One guy in there was deemed the closer. The rest were guys who couldn't start, so they were in the bullpen too.

Compare that with what they have today. There's the closer; a setup guy who pitches the eighth inning; a setup guy who sets up the setup guy and pitches the seventh. There's a long man; another short man; a guy who only gets out lefties. Managers can mix and match more effectively with those relievers than they ever could. When I was pitching, managers never had that luxury because, in general, the starters were so much better than the relievers. Heck, if I were pitching in today's game, I might only end up going six innings on most nights. Though, knowing me, I wouldn't be so happy with the manager if he came out to me that early asking for the ball.

You can see this specialization make its way down from the majors to baseball at all ages. When I went to college, you were a starter or you pitched in the bullpen because you couldn't crack it. Today in high school you might have a closer and a fully stocked bullpen. Even in Little League. Because people aren't stupid. They see what's out there, how the game is changing, and what's valued. It's something the Yankees have prioritized in recent years, building deep bullpens with the likes of Aroldis Chapman and Dellin Betances.

The other big emphasis in the game these days ties well into the modern Yankees team too. More guys are trying to hit the ball out of the park than ever before. Most of the best batters I faced had a measured approach to hitting that they took pride in. They would take one big swing early in the at-bat to hit it out. If that didn't work, their approach changed. They'd try to get a hit up the middle or to the opposite field. Or they'd try to hit the ball behind a runner.

Now these guys take three swings for the fences. I'm not faulting anybody or even saying it's a problem. But it has noticeably changed the game. Home runs are way up—2017 set the major-league record. And the consequence of that is that strikeouts are way up too. If batters aren't shortening up their swings, they get more chances to hit it out, but they also swing and miss more. Also, you can't tell me the ball ain't changed with the way it's flying off bats.

The thing is, you'll hear people gripe that all this is a problem and that it's making games take longer and ripping some of the nuance out of the sport. But I'm not too sure a lot of people in the stands, who pay a great deal of money for their seats these days, want to see a quick 1–0 game. They may want it to last, and to see five or six home runs in one sitting. Or one of Aaron Judge's mammoth home runs.

Which brings it back to this modern Yankees team with guys like Judge, the giant outfielder sensation, and Gary Sanchez, a catcher and another powerful young hitter. They have both been so successful early in their careers that it's natural for people to ask if they can form a core like Derek Jeter, Jorge Posada, and some of the others. Only time will answer that. But I think the key thing to remember about Jeter and Posada is that it wasn't just about their talent. It was their personalities and *how* they played the game.

The most remarkable aspect of that duo was how polished they were. Both off the field and in their approach to baseball. They showed up every day and took immense pride in their work. They did every little thing, from practice to warm-ups to the final out. At the plate, Jeter wouldn't just get hits. He'd move runners over. When he made outs, they were often productive outs. They had style, grace. More than anything else, from the first day they stepped onto a major-league diamond, they played like fifteen-year veterans.

Take Posada. He was a lot like Munson, in that sense of pride about mastering his job, which for a catcher is more important than any field position. The catcher calls the game for the pitcher and sets the tone. And Jorge was a great hitter, Munson was too, don't get me wrong. But both of them loved catching, *then* they loved hitting. Posada loved catching because that was his number one job.

So what's exciting for the Yankees now is that they have the potential to build the same type of young, exciting, talented team that brought all those World Series trophies to the

Bronx. Sanchez and Judge, they have incredible talent. While they have work to do to refine their games, they've already showed star power. And it's not just them. It wouldn't shock me if Greg Bird, the first baseman, turned out to be just as good or better than the rest of them. His approach at the plate is like a fifteen-year veteran's. He can make great contact and pick the right pitch. And there are more in the minors who can get there soon.

There are also the pitchers: Luis Severino showed he has the potential to be a real ace in 2017. I've always been real high on Jordan Montgomery, too, another pitcher, even though he didn't come into the season with all that much hype. There are more on the way.

All of this sets up for a future Yankees fans should be thrilled about. For years our minor-league system wasn't very good. It clearly has been these last few years. The outlook is great, so much better than it was in the mid-2000s. But just because these guys have talent and the *potential* to be that great doesn't mean anything yet. There's a lot these guys can learn in the coming years about transitioning from great players to polished ones. When they do that, the sky is the limit. It'll be fun to watch.

14

THE REAL YOGI BERRA

The world lost a giant when Yogi Berra died on September 22, 2015. If someone more beloved walked this earth, I'd like to meet that person. Baseball stars, heroes, and legends have come and gone. None has cast the long shadow that Yogi did. He connected with Yankees fans, baseball fans, and people who didn't give a flying hoot about the sport in a way *nobody* has ever done, so far as I know. Everybody dreamed of being a little bit like Yogi. Part of what made Yogi such a towering figure was that he dreamed bigger than anybody else around him.

The Yogi I'd like to tell you about is someone a little different from the person in the stories he has become famous for. Because if you have only a cursory knowledge of Lawrence Peter Berra, you might only remember him for saying some silly things. They even have their own terminology: Yogi-isms. I'm not sure how many of these he actually said (he himself said, "I never said most of the things I said") or whether or not he invented them, but Yogi-isms have come to be one of the ways he's best remembered. Sayings like:

"*Baseball is ninety percent mental; the other half is
 physical.*"
"*When you come to a fork in the road, take it.*"
"*It ain't the heat, it's the humility.*"
"*It gets late early out there.*"
"*It ain't over till it's over.*"
"*You can observe a lot just by watching.*"

Here's the thing about Yogi. There are so many things one
can take away from his life: the values of passion, hard work,
kindness, mentorship, stubbornness, righteous indignation—
the list goes on. But if I could leave you with one thing, it's
that he taught the world that the only opinion of yourself that
matters is your own. He was constantly told no in his life, and
he inevitably fought his way to yes. He was told he was too
small, yet he became the biggest man in baseball history. He
was laughed at for the way he spoke, and he grew to be one
of the most brilliant commentators the world has ever seen.
That is the legend of Yogi. He might have had a funnier way
of explaining it, but he was the most underestimated athlete
and person this great game ever saw. I was just lucky to be
friends with him.

———

Everybody has a picture or an idea about what Yogi was like,
but there's a Yogi that people don't know as well. Not Yogi the
cartoon or Yogi the lovable old man. This is Yogi the relentless, fierce, unyielding baseball player. From the very beginning, he had to overcome the fact that he did not look like a
baseball player. He did not sound like a baseball player. He
never went to school past eighth grade; the son of Italian im-

migrants, he sounded like it. He never grew past five foot seven, although it seemed as if his ears kept growing to fit the head of a man twice his size. Picture a tall, handsome, and charismatic baseball icon. Well, Yogi was the opposite.

Maybe that's why when he tried out for the Cardinals, his hometown team, he was offered half the money one of his friends received. It didn't matter that Yogi could hit a baseball farther than players who had eight inches on him. So even though he came from a humble background where every dollar meant the world to him, Yogi refused a deal from Branch Rickey, considered one of the greatest general managers to ever work in baseball. He held out until somebody signed him for what he felt he deserved. And if no team signed him, so be it. Eventually one team did just that. The New York Yankees.

And despite Yogi Berra doing pretty much everything you could ask of him—from playing in the minor leagues to serving in the U.S. Navy during the invasion of Normandy—he *still* faced doubts about whether he could make it. He hit a home run in his first major-league at-bat, yet people couldn't stop making fun of the way he swung. That was because he swung at everything. People laughed at some of his attempts. He chased breaking balls at his feet and fastballs above his head. But the funny thing is, usually folks who swing at everything end up striking out a lot. Yogi was the opposite. He was obsessed with putting his bat on the ball. During his first five years in the majors, he hit seventy-five home runs— which was one more than the number of times he struck out.

The only thing more remarkable than his uncanny hitting ability was his astonishing excellence behind the plate. Catchers are typically big. Yogi's small size and awkward, stubby build made people question whether he would last back there. Second, catchers are the brains of the club. They help align the defense. They have to know where the ball goes on any given play. Most important, they need to call the pitches. That requires a thorough knowledge of every opposing batter, and always being on the same page with your pitchers.

This is why the Yogi-isms are so comical. They were born out of this idea that Yogi was some kind of village idiot who mumbled and could barely form a sentence. The reality couldn't be further from the truth. During his prime, the Yankees pitchers wiggled their way through games despite not having a staff with particularly noteworthy or famous arms. (Whitey Ford didn't come until midway through Yogi's career.) The Yankees pitchers were always better with Yogi behind the plate. He knew exactly what pitch to call and where to set his glove. He knew when to call for the inside pitch to brush batters off. He squeezed every strike and every win out of his pitchers.

When you're able to do that, you really don't care what people say about you or how you are depicted. Yogi, the humble man he was, almost never talked about himself. But during my years as a player and instructor, I got the chance to talk with guys like Whitey, Eddie Lopat, and Vic Raschi, who got to pitch to Yogi. It was clear to me that Whitey pitching to Yogi was like me pitching to Thurman. A good pitcher becomes a great one with an outstanding catcher behind the plate. Yogi was an outstanding catcher because he was the game's ultimate thinker. Ironic, considering he was a guy people laughed at for the way he spoke. The fact was, he was smarter than everyone around him.

Those are the qualities that led him to help win ten World

Series, more than any other player in baseball history. He was the guy who was overlooked every step of the way. But he was so damn stubborn and had such passion that rejection only fueled him to greater heights. To me, that's the start of what makes him such a revered figure. One minute, he would be thoughtfully breaking down opposing batters and deciding what pitches to call. The next moment he'd be chasing an umpire around the field because he refused to accept what he perceived to be an unfair call. It's a side of Yogi, his sheer will and determination, that isn't spoken of enough.

When I was a young boy, racing home from school to catch the end of Yankees games on television, Yogi wasn't front and center. I was born in 1950, and by the time I was really following the game, Yogi was past his prime. I more closely followed the careers of Mickey, Whitey, and Roger Maris. Yogi played his last season as a Yankee, and that was only sixty-four games, in 1963.

Then, as I got older, I started to hear the stories about Yogi and the other Yankees greats. I'd read about some of the more famous old games and occasionally saw a replay of a famous moment. Then suddenly Yogi was my coach, his locker next to mine. And all the qualities he had as a player, he brought to us as a coach. He could be silly, walking around the clubhouse in his underwear, having a chew and making us laugh. He could be intense and insightful, explaining to me when I needed to throw some chin music, and how to attack batters. He covered the whole spectrum.

The toughest thing to watch was his self-imposed exile after George fired him as a manager. As I explained earlier, he said he wouldn't step in Yankee Stadium again so long as George owned the team. If anybody else said that, you'd shrug it off. But Yogi *lived* to be on the baseball field. He was born to walk on the grass; it was a shame for someone with such an in-depth knowledge of and love for the game to become so exiled from it. It was a shame for the Yankees organization to be out of touch with the guy who had won more World Series than anybody else in a Yankees uniform. Somebody who defined what it meant to be a Yankee—the gruff, working-class attitude that New Yorkers adored, the willingness to fight against any odds. Hollywood looks might not have won anything for him, but his determination did. And now, that same determination kept him away from the Yankees for nearly fifteen years.

Between the stubbornness of Yogi and the stubbornness of Mr. Steinbrenner, the only surprising thing is that their cold war ever ended. But they both loved the same thing: the New York Yankees. That's what led George to Yogi's museum in New Jersey in 1999 to apologize in person. It's the same feeling that led Yogi, a man who had vowed never to return to Yankee Stadium so long as George owned the team, to accept George's apology. Together they made plans for a grand return, a Yogi Berra Day that July. Before the game, Don Larsen, the Yankees pitcher who threw the first perfect game in Yankees history, during the 1956 World Series with Yogi behind the plate, tossed the ceremonial first pitch to Yogi. A few hours later David Cone finished another perfect game, the third in the team's history. As if we needed another sign that all was right in the world.

The end of that feud meant something special to me. Yogi Berra would return to spring training. The man born to wear a Yankees uniform would be coming to Tampa (our facilities had moved from Fort Lauderdale by then) to be involved in the game and the team once again. I couldn't wait. I loved every second spent around the guy. I didn't know, however, just how close we'd become. For I became Yogi Berra's chauffeur.

It all happened very organically. I had told him after the reconciliation that if he came to spring training, I'd pick him up. And once you tell Yogi something, that's how it goes. It started with scooping him up from the airport in my truck. From there, it slowly evolved. He had a simple rule: "Don't be late, Gator." I'd take him grocery shopping. I'd shuttle him to and from the hotel. We'd go out to dinner every night. Until we'd eat out so much that I'd insist on cooking up some frog legs or something because there are only so many damn times you can eat out. Although one of the benefits of going around town with Yogi Berra is that you rarely have to pay for your meals. More than you'd think, we'd ask for the check and the waiter would say it had been covered. What?

"Mr. Guidry, Mr. Berra, you see that couple over there? Yogi smiled and waved at them earlier, and they were so appreciative they wanted to treat him to a meal."

When Reggie would see us together, he'd call me Yogi's "guide dog." Going around town with him was like traveling with the pope. We'd get out of the car somewhere, and cars would literally stop in the middle of the road so people could honk their horns or open their doors and wave. And Yogi was so gracious about all of it. He never ran out of smiles and *almost* never got upset with the crowds at restaurants. Maybe once he felt overwhelmed and then we just found a new restaurant to eat at. Those fans had given him the greatest gift in the world, a family that loved him and cheered him and made Yankee Stadium a home, and he never forgot that. After Yogi's funeral, his sons joked to me that whenever they offered to give him a ride or grab supper with him during those times, he'd tell them, "Sorry, Gator is taking us out."

It wasn't just me who loved having Yogi around. The players *loved* it. They'd enjoy busting his chops because Yogi was old-school and he liked hobnobbing with everyone just like he was one of the guys, even though everyone knew he was more than that—a legend. But that's how he wanted it. To joke around and be joked around with.

But he wasn't just some sort of mascot, either. He still had the brilliant eye for baseball, teaching the game that made him so great. Players would pick his brain and they got invaluable lessons. It was great for them, and it was great for Yogi, too. It made him feel important. Not in some patronizing way, because the reality was that he *was* important.

During the games, he and I always sat on the same spots on the bench, right by the entrance to the clubhouse. The bat racks were on one side, then the bins for the bubble gum, then a couple of coolers with the water and Gatorade. We sat next to those, and he'd lean against the coolers if he needed. We sat there all game and he'd share his observations. Even in his later years, they were keen as ever. He noticed everything.

One game, we were watching as Nick Swisher, who was on the Yankees from 2009 to 2012, stepped to the plate. He was facing a sinkerballer, and he weakly grounded out to the left side. Second time he comes up, same thing. Weak ground ball. "Why doesn't he either move up in the batter's box or get closer to the plate so he can get a better swing on that type of pitch?" Yogi said to me.

"What the hell are you telling me for? Tell him!"

Yogi laughed. "Oh no, I don't wanna bother those kids."

The next night, we're facing the same type of pitcher.

We're sitting on the bench watching as Swisher takes his first at-bat. He does the same thing, weak contact, and gets out. Again, Yogi didn't feel it was his place to say something. Swisher comes back to the dugout, puts his helmet in its spot and his bat in the rack. As he gets set to walk past us I stand up and put a hand on his shoulder. I tell him to sit in my seat and to listen to Yogi. He does just that.

"Swish," Yogi said, "what type of pitcher is that?"

"Sinkerballer," Swisher said.

"You should either move up in the batter's box or move closer to the plate to where you can get a better swing at it, before it starts to break and run. You'd get a better swing at it."

They spoke for a few minutes and Swisher got up, clearly taking in what Yogi said. Sure enough, next time Swisher was up he cranked one of those sinkers off the left-center-field wall. Now, whenever Swisher got a big hit he'd point to the sky to honor his grandmother. So he did that. Then he started pointing right at Yogi. I elbowed Yogi; he saw and he got a kick out of it. Then, when Swisher came back into the dugout, he ran in and thanked Yogi for the tip.

I love what Swish said after. "I'd quit playing if I had the opportunity like you to sit next to him all game."

When you spend enough time with Yogi, you learn that the Yogi-isms are based in reality. He'd just say something that would stop you in your tracks—or in this case, made me stop my car because I was laughing so damn hard. One time I had to drive Yogi to the airport in Florida. You could tell if Yogi was in a good mood by whether or not he was waving, and this day he wasn't. He got into my truck cussing up a storm.

"What's the problem?" I asked. He grumbled something about having to fly out to Los Angeles to film an "affliction" commercial. I had no idea what the heck he was talking about. Was it about cancer? Or some medicine? What in the world is an affliction commercial?

"You know," he snorted, "with that damn duck."

I had to pull over, I was laughing so damn hard. "Aflac!" I said. Then he realized. He started laughing too. But what was funnier was what happened when I picked him up on the way back. He sauntered on out of the terminal and into my truck and offered this big revelation.

"Gator, you realize that duck doesn't really talk?"

But for every one of those stories about Yogi, there are dozens more about what he was like as a player and coach. The complete collection is why he's so beloved. And for a guy who won three MVPs and ten World Series titles and went to fifteen All-Star Games, he talked as if he hadn't accomplished a damn thing in his entire career. The only way you could get him to talk about himself was to ask about other people, and he'd have to mention himself in the process. What was it like to catch Larsen's perfect game? To play for Casey Stengel? To bat against Sandy Koufax? Ask something like that, over dinner or on a car ride, and you could sit back and listen for hours.

And no matter how old he got, you could still get flashes of the fiery competitor that made him who he was. My favorite way to do that was to bring up the 1955 World Series, which the Dodgers went on to win against Yogi and the Yankees in seven games. The way to get him riled up was to bring up game one, which the Yankees won despite a call that Yogi had never gotten over even half a century later. During the eighth inning of that game, Jackie Robinson stole home on a Whitey Ford delivery and got underneath Yogi's tag. Or so said the home-plate umpire. Yogi was furious. He got just as angry every instance he was coaxed into retelling the story. The stubbornness that made him so great never subsided.

A few years ago he signed a picture of the play for President Barack Obama:

Dear Mr. President,
He was out!
Yogi Berra.

————

When I began going to spring training as an instructor, George said, "I'd like you to come as long as you enjoy it." After ten years, I was still enjoying it. But I began to ask myself, "How much longer will I continue to love it and keep doing it?" Maybe twenty years, I thought. That long, I told myself, would feel like a real accomplishment, like you've done something good for a long time. All of a sudden, just like that, I get to twenty years and I'm packing my truck and going down again. Then I'm telling myself, "Wait a minute, I was looking at twenty, and now I'm at twenty-five." That's unusual for me. When I say to myself "This is it," that's usually it.

By this time, Yogi had stopped coming to spring training. He was physically unable to go. He was back home, had been feeling on and off, good and bad. Some days Joni Bronander from Yogi's museum, who'd look after him, would call and say he's doing good today, so I should call him. So I'd do that, and we'd talk and it'd be great.

About a month before Yogi passed in 2015, I was headed up to New York after spring training for various events and found that I had a full day free. So it dawned on me that I'm doing nothing that day, and the Yankees were playing a day game, so I ought to surprise Yogi. We'll get something to eat, watch the game, and it'll be great. So I call Joni, set it all up but tell her not to tell him about it. Keep it a surprise. She said she knew this place where Yogi loved the cheeseburgers; she'd pick some up for us.

So I drive there that day, and she pokes her head into Yogi's room. He's sitting in bed. "Look what I found in the hall," she says. He turned his head, and I walk in.

"Hey, buddy, what's happenin'," I said. Oh, the big smile he got on his face! He sat up in bed; I walked over, gave him a hug and a kiss on the cheek. We start talking, and I tell him I'm here to watch the game with him. Then his face lit up even more when Joni told him he was getting those cheeseburgers and fries he loves. "Oh, that little place down the road makes 'em good," he said.

So we sat there and watched the game just like we would've on the bench all those years ago. An inning or so in, somebody came to take Yogi to meet with the physical therapist—well, Yogi wasn't having that.

Then, during the game, the conversation on the broadcast turned to me and Yogi. Whoever was hitting at the time accidentally flung his bat into the dugout while he was swinging and guys had to scatter all over the place. There had been an instance in spring training a few years before where the exact same thing happened.

At that time, Yogi and I were sitting in the dugout and the bat came flying in, twirling right at us. I jumped up in front to make sure the bat didn't hit him. When it reached us, it just grazed me on the kneecap. It stung but wasn't anything

THE REAL YOGI BERRA 217

noteworthy. But what was amazing was seeing the entire team come over and make sure everything was all right. They didn't care if I was okay, of course, they wanted to make sure Yogi was okay . . . even though the bat didn't hit him. So the announcers were laughing about that because the whole affair—me jumping in front, and everybody checking on Yogi even though the bat didn't hit him—was a testament to how everyone cared so much about Yogi.

To take a step back, earlier in 2015, before I had gone to New York to see Yogi, I had spoken with Joe Girardi, the Yankees manager at the time, and said it was probably my last year of coming to spring training. He protested, of course. Joe always loved having us around and treated us great. "No, no, no," he said.

"Look, guys. I've been coming since 1990 as a coach, I'm over sixty years old, I think I'd like to stay home. I haven't seen a Louisiana February since 1972. It's been on my mind, and I think it's time." Joe said he'd call me next year anyway. Deep down inside, I had made my decision and I thought that was that.

So when they started recounting that story on the telecast about the bat during spring training, I said to Yogi, "Well, that's never going to happen to me again."

"What do you mean?" Yogi asked. So I told him that I had talked with Joe about that spring being my last spring.

Yogi sat up in his bed as much as he could. I was in a chair next to him. The moment suddenly grew very intense. He looked at me intently. "Oh no. You've got to go."

"What?"

"Oh no," he repeated. "You've got to keep going."

"Why in the hell do I gotta keep going?"

"Because," he said, "I won't be able to go."

That turn of phrase—"I won't be able to go"—it struck me. I didn't know if he meant physically. Did he mean that he couldn't go? Or he was not going to be around to go?

"Yogi," I said. "I might go a couple more years."

Then I leaned over and cracked a big smile. "But I will tell you this: I'm not going until I'm over eighty years old like you." Then he started laughing. The tension was over. But I kept thinking about what he was saying.

And it's why I continued going even after his passing a month later. If I stop going, does all of it stop? Would Goose stop going? Who's gonna take your place? But in the last couple of years, more and more of the younger—and when I say younger, I mean relative to me—guys have started to come, which is great. Orlando "El Duque" Hernandez, Andy Pettitte, Mariano Rivera, Jorge Posada, Bernie Williams, and others. Which is great. Because you know, I know, we know, that all of these stories, lessons, and rich tradition that all distinctly belong to the New York Yankees . . . they'll continue.

ACKNOWLEDGMENTS

There have been so many times when we've all been together and someone asks: Did all of that really happen? Yes, it did.

I have so many people to thank for this book, but for that reason the first people I would like to acknowledge are the Yankees and my incredible teammates. All of these stories, and all of this great history, we lived through it together. Mr. Steinbrenner and the Yankees took a chance on a string bean from Louisiana and I could not be more grateful. The organization has continued to be a family for me, and so many others, even since my retirement—which is just the greatest testament to the class of the Steinbrenner family, the front office, and everyone who has welcomed us back every season. Once a Yankee, always a Yankee. There is nothing like it.

I also need to thank everyone who put on the pinstripes with me. There are so many people to list that it would take pages upon pages. Everything that happened, we learned from, persevered through, and experienced together. There are those like Thurman Munson, Sparky Lyle, and Dick Tidrow, who could teach me more about pitching—and life—in one clubhouse conversation than I'd expert to learn in an entire season. I have a special appreciation for others such as Goose Gossage, who went on to be and remain lifelong friends; and Willie Randolph, my longtime teammate and friend who I had the special privilege of being co-captains with.

So many of these teammates have written incredible books that are invaluable recollections of history for anybody who wants to relive this era and understand what it means to be a Yankee. To name a couple: *The Bronx Zoo* by Sparky Lyle and *Lou: Fifty Years of Kicking Dirt, Playing Hard, and Winning Big in the Sweet Spot of Baseball* by Lou Piniella both captured profound memories and emotion. The number of Yankees books by others is vast too, but I also especially appreciated *Driving Mr. Yogi* by Harvey Araton that focused on Yogi Berra and our friendship, a bond that means so much to me. I am also indebted to the newspaper writers who covered us every day from organizations like the *New York Times,* the *Daily News,* and the *New York Post;* those big headlines may have been big headaches for us amid all the drama, but those articles and pictures are also important records of our Yankees history.

Finally, and most importantly, I cannot express enough gratitude to my family. My loving, passionate, and brilliant wife, Bonnie, supported me in times good and bad. She was there for advice, comfort, and counsel. Without Bonnie, none of this would have ever happened. That brings me to my children: Jamie, Brandon, and Danielle. They know my stories as well as I do at this point. Along with Bonnie, they helped me read through the pages of this book and help bring it to where it is today. We recounted old stories and shared laughs. We pored through old pictures that brought back even more memories. They didn't only always support me and make me the proudest father in the world, but they also were a constant reminder of what's important in life. And the way I was raised, nothing means more to me than family.

INDEX

About the Authors

RON GUIDRY is one of the most beloved players in Yankees history. The ace of the Yankees pitching staff from 1977 through 1988, Guidry helped the Yankees win two World Series titles. Captain of the Yankees squad in the 1980s, he spent his entire career in pinstripes. Since retirement he has served as a Yankees spring training instructor and was the Yankees pitching coach under Joe Torre in 2006–2007, helping to shape a new generation of pitching stars. He lives with his family in Louisiana.

ANDREW BEATON is a sports reporter for the *Wall Street Journal*. A graduate of Duke University, he has covered college sports, baseball, and the National Football League.